FAST SCRAPBOOKING
with 4x6 Photos

SCRAPBOOK YOUR PHOTOS STRAIGHT FROM THE PRINTER!

ButterFly KiSSeS

Kendall Loves Getting Butterfly Kisses at the Butterfly Pavilion

A LEISURE ARTS PUBLICATION

CREATIVE CRAFTS GROUP, LLC.

President and CEO
Stephen J. Kent

VP/Group Publisher
Tina Battock

President of Book Publishing
W. Budge Wallis

Chief Financial Officer
Mark F. Arnett

Corporate Controller
Jordan Bohrer

VP/Publishing Director
Joel P. Toner

VP/Production
Barbara Schmitz

VP/Circulation
Nicole McGuire

Associate Publisher
Barb Tanner

Production Manager
Michael Rueckwald

Production Coordinator
Erin Sendelbach

CREATING KEEPSAKES

Editor-in-Chief
Jennafer Martin

Founding Editor
Lisa Bearnson

Managing Editor
Lara Penrod

Creative Editor
Megan Hoeppner

Senior Editor
Kim Jackson

Editor
Lori Fairbanks

Associate Editor
Joannie McBride

Copy Editor
Sara Peterson

Online Senior Editor
Amber Ellis

Online Editor
Erin Weed

Editorial Assistant
Ahtanya Johnson

Contributing Writer
Maurianne Dunn

Art Director
Erin Bayless

Senior Designer
Neko Carillo

Contributing Designer
Gaige Redd

Photography
BPD Studios, Vertis Communications

LEISURE ARTS

Vice President and Editor-in-Chief
Susan White Sullivan

Director of Designer Relations
Cheryl Johnson

Special Projects Director
Susan Frantz Wiles

Senior Prepress Director
Mark Hawkins

Imaging Technician
Stephanie Johnson

Prepress Technician
Janie Marie Wright

Publishing Systems Administrator
Becky Riddle

Mac Information Technology Specialist
Robert Young

President and Chief Executive Officer
Rick Barton

Vice President of Sales
Mike Behar

Director of Finance and Administration
Laticia Mull Dittrich

National Sales Director
Martha Adams

Creative Services
Chaska Lucas

Information Technology Director
Hermine Linz

Controller
Francis Caple

Vice President, Operations
Jim Dittrich

Retail Customer Service Manager
Stan Raynor

Print Production Manager
Fred F. Pruss

Published by Leisure Arts, Inc., 5701 Ranch Drive, Little Rock, Arkansas 72223-9633. 501-868-8800. www.leisurearts.com.

This product is manufactured under license for Creative Crafts Group, LLC, Creative Crafts Group company, publisher of Creating Keepsakes® scrapbook magazine. ©2012. All rights reserved.

Library of Congress Control Number: 2011941160
ISBN-13/EAN: 978-1-60900-383-8

GET IT DONE TODAY

There's nothing quite like the satisfaction that comes from completing a scrapbook page. Seeing your photos and journaling creatively paired with your favorite paper and accents brings a sense of pride and joy unlike any other. Unfortunately, sometimes these feelings are elusive because we get caught up spending more time fussing with our photos than scrapbooking them. Saving time on that part of scrapbooking is where this book comes in handy. In the pages that follow, you'll see hundreds of little-to-no-cropping-required scrapbook layouts and albums to save you time. Following the ideas in this book, you'll be able to

- increase the number of times you feel that layout-completion pride by creating layouts using photos straight from the printer,

- use the time you may usually spend cropping or resizing photos to complete more layouts,

- save money you may have spent on photo enlargement prints to spend on more of your favorite scrapbooking supplies,

- gain inspiration to create countless layouts, cards, gifts, and albums, and

- learn easy design tips for creatively and beautifully showcasing 4" x 6" photos on your layouts.

We hope you find ideas in this issue you'll use frequently to save time, complete more scrapbook pages, and experience that layout-completion pride again and again!

JENNAFER MARTIN
Editor-in-Chief

Fast Scrapbooking with 4 x 6 Photos

CONTENTS

SAVE TIME THE SUPER-FAST WAY

My Story | Lisa Bearnson

Patterned Paper: Scenic Route; *Rivets*: Chatterbox;
Brackets and journaling card: Teresa Collins Designs;
Pen: American Crafts.

I recently discovered the joy of super-fast scrapbooking. Now don't get me wrong—I've loved all the creative hours I've spent assembling pages over the years. But I found myself getting bogged down with resizing photos and printing them both on my own personal printer and at the photo lab. The process was taking valuable time that I would rather spend making and preserving memories.

Now I simply take my photo card to my favorite photo lab, print the majority of my photos in a 4" x 6" format, and then file them away for later use. When I'm ready to create a page, I just grab the photos I want to use and finish my design in stellar time. And with the ideas in this issue, I'm scrapbooking even faster—all the layouts featured inside are created with uncropped 4" x 6" photos!

Fast Scrapbooking with 4 x 6 Photos is broken down into six chapters based on the number of photos. We've also added some fun sidebars with techniques you can use with your photos, like journaling in the white space, layering photos, adding a frame over the top and so on. You'll love these great ideas for enhancing your 4" x 6" pictures.

Have fun with the process, and keep taking lots of photos along the way. Even better, enjoy the extra time you have for making memories!

Lisa Bearnson

10 SHORTCUTS
for Fast and Beautiful Pages

CREATE THESE PAGES FAST WITH 4" X 6" PHOTOS.

WHEN WAS THE LAST TIME YOU SPENT HOURS AT YOUR computer resizing photos to get that perfect look on your page, or you used your scrapbook time to crop 4" x 6" prints with your trimmer? While these cropping techniques are great on some pages, sometimes you want a quick page design where you don't have to crop or resize anything. So go get a few pages done using the following 10 pages as inspiration—all of the photos are 4" x 6" pictures straight from the printer.

BY Maurianne Dunn

SHORTCUT
1

Use pre-glittered and pre-embossed patterned papers.

Instead of spending time embossing or glittering her layout, Mou Saha used specialty glitter paper. Using these types of papers adds a lot of pizzazz quickly.

Pumpkin Carving 101 *by Mou Saha.* **Supplies** *Cardstock:* Die Cuts With a View; *Patterned paper and rub-ons:* Piggy Tales; *Stickers:* Heidi Swapp for Advantus (block numbers) and Piggy Tales (title); *Rhinestones:* Rusty Pickle; *Pen:* American Crafts; *Adhesive:* Scotch, 3M.

Design tip: A mirrored image doesn't have to be perfectly symmetrical. Notice how Melissa Deakin put a photo on the bottom of her left-hand page while adding it to the top of the right-hand page. The overall feeling is still symmetrical and balanced, but the slight twist adds brilliance to the design.

SHORTCUT
2

Mirror Your Pages.

If you're looking for a quick page design, make the right-hand page of your layout mirror the left-hand page. Melissa Deakin used the same patterned paper on both sides of the layout to frame the photos, and she used the same border strips next to her photos as well—it's so simple but so beautiful!

Nope *by Melissa Deakin.* **Supplies** *Cardstock:* Bazzill Basics Paper (yellow) and The Paper Company (cream); *Patterned paper:* Heather Bailey for Autumn Leaves; *Software:* Adobe Photoshop 7.0; *Font:* American Typewriter Light; *Adhesive:* Mono Adhesive, Tombow.

SHORTCUT #3

Use brads instead of adhesive.

Cindy Tobey used brads to adhere a felt spiderweb accent to her layout by placing brads in the center of each web. This is an easy way to adhere shaped felt without the fuss of wet adhesive. Try it with vellum, fabric, ribbon or patterned paper as well!

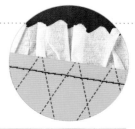

Feeling the Force by Cindy Tobey. **Supplies** *Cardstock:* Bazzill Basics Paper (yellow) and Prism Paper (black); *Patterned paper:* Crate Paper (green circle), KI Memories (orange stripe), Making Memories (orange diamond and black) and My Mind's Eye (green solid); *Ink:* Clearsnap; *Brads:* Queen & Co.; *Stickers:* KI Memories; *Spider stickers:* Little Yellow Bicycle; *Chipboard:* BasicGrey (letters) and Melissa Frances (pumpkin); *Journaling tag:* Heidi Swapp for Advantus; *Felt:* Martha Stewart Crafts; *Crepe paper ribbon:* Jenni Bowlin Studio; *Mesh:* Glitz Design; *Marker:* Sakura; *Adhesive:* 3M, Glue Dots International and Tombow; *Other:* Thread.

How-To: Easy Ruffle Borders

Ruffled tissue borders are easier than they look! Follow these steps to create the look in under a minute:

❶ Run a line of adhesive where you want the border.

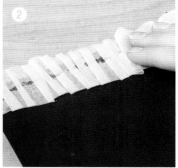

❷ Pleat a strip of tissue paper along the adhesive, gathering as you go.

Try cutting strips from gift-wrap tissue or crepe-paper streamers, or check out crepe paper from one of these companies:

Crepe Paper
Melissa Frances
MelissaFrances.com

Crepe Paper Ribbon
Jenni Bowlin Studio
JenniBowlin.com

Group your photos around the center of the layout.

One difficulty with using 4" x 6" photos is finding a way to fit them all on the layout while also including embellishments. Pam Callaghan's solution is to group your photos around the center of the layout and surround them with color and text. It helps keep the focus on what's most important: the photos.

7th Birthday Party *by Pam Callaghan.* **Supplies** *Cardstock:* Anna Griffin (kraft), Bazzill Basics Paper (white) and Die Cuts With a View (red); *Patterned paper:* Anna Griffin (green), Bo-Bunny Press (stripe, balloons and "birthday"), CherryArte (blue mini-dot) and Creative Imaginations (scalloped, blue dot and orange); *Stickers:* Anna Griffin (red), Creative Imaginations (label) and Scenic Route (black); *Ink:* Anna Griffin; *Embroidery floss:* DMC; *Die-cutting machine:* Slice, Making Memories; *Font:* Bangle.

How-To: Easy Balloon Accents

Balloon accents are fun to include on layouts for many different celebrations. Here are two easy ways to create them for your layout:

Option 2:
Punch and Adhere

❶ Use a circle punch to create a round shape.

❷ Adhere a small tab to the circle.

❸ Tie a piece of string or embroidery floss around the tab.

Option 1: *Cut by Hand*

❶ Draw a circle shape with a small tab on one side; cut out.

❷ Tie a piece of string or embroidery floss around the tab.

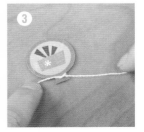

Download and print a free journaling block.

Kelly Goree wanted to include a talk bubble on her layout (it reinforces the comic-book theme). Rather than spend time drawing the perfect shape, she searched for "talk bubble" on the Internet and downloaded an image. Once printed, the talk bubble served as the perfect home for her title.

Holy Costume, Batman! *by Kelly Goree.* **Supplies** *Cardstock:* Bazzill Basics Paper (black and white) and SEI (purple); *Patterned paper:* BasicGrey (orange, stripe and orange bat) and SEI (green bat); *Bat die cuts, tags and chipboard letters:* BasicGrey; *Ink:* ColorBox, Clearsnap; *Flax string:* Scrapworks; *Talk bubble:* Internet; *Pen:* Pentel; *Font:* International Super Hero; *Adhesive:* Scrapbook Adhesives by 3L.

SHORTCUT
#6

Use quick-and-easy embellishments.

Maggie Holmes incorporated embellishments that are quick and easy to use but add a lot of impact: die-cut stickers, border strips, buttons and brads.

Oct. '06 *by Maggie Holmes.* **Supplies** *Cardstock:* Wausau Paper; *Patterned paper:* Jenni Bowlin Studio (die cut), Sassafras (stripe and squirrel) and Studio Calico (yellow, green floral, orange, red stripe and tan); *Brads:* Heidi Swapp for Advantus; *Stickers:* American Crafts (letters), Making Memories (pebble) and Sassafras (decorative); *Chipboard:* American Crafts; *Fabric strips:* Studio Calico; *Rhinestones:* me & my BIG ideas; *Buttons:* Making Memories; *Scallop scissors:* Fiskars Americas; *Pen:* Slick Writers, American Crafts; *Adhesive:* Dot 'n' Roller, Kokuyo; Zots, Therm O Web.

Punch borders from paper scraps.

Kim Watson puts her border punches to good use. Whenever she has paper scraps left over, she uses border punches to create beautiful borders for future layouts. Now she has a drawer full of decorative border strips made from paper that would have otherwise gone straight to the trash.

Touch *by Kim Watson.* **Supplies** *Cardstock:* American Crafts (dark orange), Bazzill Basics Paper (red and white) and Die Cuts With a View (light orange and pink); *Patterned paper:* Kaisercraft (orange heart), K&Company (glitter strips), Pebbles Inc. (floral), Pink Paislee (yellow) and Sassafras (frames); *Die-cut paper:* SEI; *Flower:* Prima; *Fabric brad:* Sassafras; *Letter stickers:* American Crafts; *Butterfly punch:* Marvy Uchida; *Pen:* Pentel; *Adhesive:* Mono Adhesive, Tombow; Scrapbook Adhesives by 3L; *Other:* Thread and typewriter. *Note:* Most supplies are from a Cocoa Daisy kit.

Color Solution: While turning on the computer may not sound like a quick solution, it can actually save you time because you can select any colors to coordinate with your layout. It's much faster than searching for the perfect color of letter stickers (or heading to the store to find them) or inking or painting a different color of letter to create the perfect match for your pages.

Use your computer.

While sticker and rub-on letters are so much fun to use, sometimes you want to put together your title a little faster. Kelly Purkey designed her title on the computer so she didn't have to worry about lining up stickers or rub-ons. With numerous fonts available for download, this is an easy alternative.

Levain Bakery *by Kelly Purkey.* **Supplies** *Cardstock:* American Crafts; *Patterned paper:* American Crafts (stripe) and Cosmo Cricket (floral); *Chipboard flowers:* Cosmo Cricket; *Gems:* Hero Arts; *Software:* Adobe Creative Suite 3; *Punches and adhesive:* Fiskars Americas; *Fonts:* AL Post Master and Metroscript.

Use scrap paper for a template.

Brenda Hurd drew a simple border around the top of her layout that unifies everything. To do this, she took a scrap piece of paper, punched one corner with a corner-rounder punch and then traced around the paper onto her layout. She flipped the paper over to create the outline on the other page. It's a simple solution with a lot of impact!

Design Tip
Because there isn't a lot of room when working with 4" x 6" photos, Brenda chose four photos with the same orientation and lined them up. This approach was easier than trying to figure out how to stagger the photos on the pages, and it allows room to easily add embellishments around the edges of the photos.

Fun in the Fall by Brenda Hurd. **Supplies** Cardstock: Prism Papers; Patterned paper, rub-ons, flowers, letter stickers and buttons: Fancy Pants Designs; Leaves: Prima; Die cuts: Collage Press; Pen: Zig, EK Success; Adhesive: Adhesive Technologies, Inc. and Glue Dots International.

Paint with ink.

Instead of getting out the paint and brushes that, while fun, generally make a mess and require cleanup, Mandy Douglass used an inkpad to change the color of her chipboard letters.

Daddy's Little Boy by Mandy Douglass. **Supplies** Cardstock, brads and letter stickers: American Crafts; Patterned paper and stickers: Pebbles Inc.; Ink: Stampin' Up!; Frame die cut: Sizzix; Circle punches: Fiskars Americas (small) and Marvy Uchida (large); Font: Century Gothic; Adhesive: Scrapbook Adhesives by 3L.

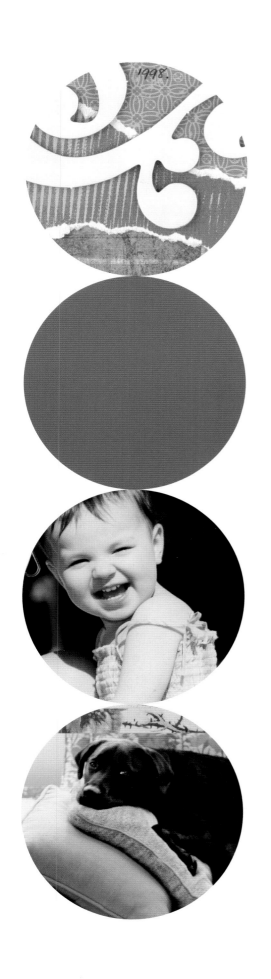

layouts with

1 TO 2

photos

Woot Woot | Kelly Purkey

Supplies *Cardstock, stickers and pen:* American Crafts; *Patterned paper:* American Crafts (green stripe) and Cosmo Cricket (floral and multi-stripe); *Rhinestones:* Hero Arts; *Punches and adhesive:* Fiskars Americas; *Other:* Thread

All hail the **POWER** of punches! Align patterned paper on white cardstock in a square, rounding the upper-left corners. Double-mat on brown and blue papers. Punch red cardstock with a border punch and adhere, then stitch to the page. Add photo, a journaling strip, punched **CARDSTOCK** hearts and rhinestones. Trim a strip of white cardstock and round the left top and bottom corners. Finish with a title.

FINISH IT FASTER!
Line up punched hearts in a pretty row.

Share | Laina Lamb

Supplies *Cardstock:* Die Cuts With a View; *Patterned paper:* Collage Press; *Stickers:* Jenni Bowlin Studio and Making Memories; *Flowers and letter stickers:* American Crafts; *Ribbon:* Creative Café, Creative Imaginations; *Stamp:* OfficeMax; *Brads and staples:* Making Memories; *Page pebbles:* The Robin's Nest; *Felt:* Heidi Swapp for Advantus; *Punch:* Fiskars Americas; *Buttons:* Li'l Davis Designs, Fiskars Americas; *Adhesive:* 3M and All Night Media; *Other:* Thread and clock element.

FINISH IT FASTER!

Do a fancy machine-stitch on just one corner of your photo.

Select a ledger background paper to make lining up paper strips and photo a **BREEZE**. Add a quick **JOURNALING** block (raised on adhesive dots), captivate with a few playful touches and you're done!

I'm with the Band | Ashley Sipple

Supplies *Cardstock:* Bazzill Basics Paper; *Patterned paper, punch-out title, phrases, butterfly, circles, photo corners, stars, tabs and ribbon slide:* Colorbök; *Acrylic scallop border:* KI Memories; *Silk flower:* Making Memories; *Ribbon:* American Crafts (star) and Hobby Lobby (white stitch); *Pen:* Newell Rubbermaid; *Adhesive:* All Night Media and Fiskars Americas. **Bright ideas:** Layer ribbon! The star ribbon here is adhered atop white-stitched ribbon. To adapt this kit for a boy page, simply include masculine accents, add more green, and place a star over the heart on the drum.

FINISH IT FASTER!
Use a kit for high-speed scrapping.

Coordinated products give your page instant cohesiveness. **PLAY** around a bit with photos, ribbons and embellishments to determine the best placement, then adhere them to the background paper. Bend butterfly **WINGS** up slightly for "lift." Place adhesive dots below both the butterfly and the title block for dimension.

Couch | Lisa Kisch

Supplies *Patterned paper:* FontWerks and Scenic Route; *Fleur de lis:* Label Tulip; *Border stickers:* Making Memories and My Mind's Eye; *Felt ribbon:* Queen & Co.; *Journaling spots:* Heidi Swapp for Advantus, Making Memories and Maya Road; *Letter stickers:* Adornit - Carolee's Creations, American Crafts and Making Memories; *Pen and adhesive:* Creative Memories. **Bright idea:** Base both your page topic and your title on the subject's point of view.

FINISH IT FASTER!
Combine two journaling spots to create a fast photo frame.

Highlight your photo by placing it on a **DECORATIVE** frame adhered to a larger piece of patterned paper. After positioning the piece on a larger background, add border **STICKERS**, felt ribbon, a title and strips with journaling.

20 Gotha Street, Camphill, Brisbane

It was run down and we paid only

$113,500 for it, but to us it was perfect.

We worked so hard doing it up – every

weekend, striping wallpaper, painting

and working in the garden

We only ended up living here for less than

two years, but it will always have a special

place in my heart, because it was ....

our first house

Our First House | Kim Arnold

Supplies *Patterned paper:* Chatterbox, Collage Press and Little Yellow Bicycle; *Chipboard and stickers:* Inque Boutique; *Letter stickers:* Adornit - Carolee's Creations; *Font:* Arial; *Adhesive:* Mono Adhesive, Tombow. **Bright idea:** Use flocked background paper to add a warm, homey touch.

Cut, tear and layer **PIECES** of paper to create a charming backdrop for photos. The hollow circle portion here is ½" thick (punch out and place the center section aside to use on another layout). Top off the page with journaling **STRIPS**, a flourish and stickers.

FINISH IT FASTER!
Sand a photo's edges for—presto—instant style.

Notes for Nana | Lisa Kisch

Supplies *Patterned paper:* My Mind's Eye and Rusty Pickle; *Chipboard letters:* BasicGrey; *Ribbon:* Making Memories; *Felt flower and rhinestone:* Chatterbox; *Decorative clip and craft wire:* Dollarama; *Font:* Century Gothic; *Adhesive:* Creative Memories; *Other:* Library card. **Bright idea:** Write pertinent details in the "Lent to:" section of a library card.

Jump-start **JOURNALING** by writing a letter from the subject's point of view. Detail both likes and dislikes. Next, mat the journaling on patterned paper. Tilt the photo nearby, then overlay the side with **RIBBON**. Add a chipboard title, replacing the letter "o" in "notes" with a rhinestone-centered felt flower.

FINISH IT FASTER!
Skip the wire on the title.

Fresh | Emily Spahn

Supplies *Cardstock:* Archiver's (kraft) and Stampin' Up! (red); *Patterned paper:* Pink Paislee; *Ribbon:* American Crafts (green) and Michaels (black); *Letter stickers:* American Crafts (title) and Making Memories (journaling); *Flower:* Heidi Swapp for Advantus; *Corner-rounder punch:* EK Success; *Pen:* Zig Writer, EK Success; *Adhesive:* Mono Adhesive, Tombow; *Other:* Ink, pin and staples.

FINISH IT FASTER!
Secure ribbon and flowers in seconds with staples.

Achieve a **FRESH** look with layering. Arrange the patterned paper and cardstock (round three of the corners on the cardstock). Mat two photos on a piece of cardstock, then round one corner. Tie two contrasting ribbons to the layout and attach them with staples. Connect the ribbons with a **SASSY** pin.

Happy Together | Emily Spahn

Supplies *Cardstock and ink:* Stampin' Up!; *Patterned paper:* K&Company (dark green), Making Memories (aqua dots), October Afternoon (red), SEI (aqua floral), Scenic Route (ledger) and Stampin' Up! (light green); *Stickers:* Doodlebug Design (letter) and Scenic Route (journaling); *Brads and photo turns:* American Crafts; *Flower:* Creative Café, Creative Imaginations; *Pen:* Zig Writer, EK Success; *Adhesive:* 3-D Dots, EK Success; Mono Adhesive, Tombow; *Other:* Button. **Bright idea:** Turn your title for added interest.

FINISH IT FASTER!
Simplify—stick with three main colors.

Layer patterned papers on your layout, giving each ample space. Outline or ink the edges for a sweet vintage appeal, then **CURL** the bottom of a larger section if desired. Outline photos and place them just off **CENTER** before adding a title and embellishments.

Sleepyhead | Lisa Truesdell

Supplies *Cardstock:* Bazzill Basics Paper; *Patterned paper:* BasicGrey (bees, pink and yellow) and Making Memories (ledger and stripe); *Overlay:* Hambly Screen Prints; *Stickers:* BasicGrey (die-cut) and Making Memories (letters); *Butterflies:* Mellette Berezoski Design; *Rhinestones:* Art Warehouse, Creative Imaginations; *Border punch:* Fiskars Americas; *Other:* Thread. **Bright idea:** Trim leftover transparency pieces into quick accent strips.

FINISH IT FASTER!
Skip the strips—use one journaling block under the photos.

Copy this great design for two similar vertical photos. **ATTACH** a large rectangle of patterned paper to a cardstock background. Add a title and stitch through both papers. Create an eye-catching vertical band with two strips of **PATTERNED** paper (use a border punch on one). Mat one photo to make it more prominent.

Island Park | Brianne McBride

Supplies *Cardstock:* The Paper Company; *Patterned paper:* Daisy Bucket Designs; *Cork letter stickers:* Making Memories; *Handmade flowers:* Petaloo; *Circle punch:* Fiskars Americas; *Pen:* Newell Rubbermaid; *Adhesive:* Glue Dots International; *Other:* Button and tag.

Talk about easy-peasy—just **ADHERE** the patterned paper to cardstock, add photos, tag, and finish the page with **FLOWERS**, title and journaling.

FINISH IT FASTER!
Use coordinated patterned-paper designs.

Are We There Yet? | Mou Saha

Supplies *Cardstock:* Die Cuts With a View; *Patterned paper:* Cosmo Cricket and Rusty Pickle; *Stickers:* American Crafts (letters), 7gypsies and Making Memories (cardstock); *Stamps:* Maya Road (ticket) and Scenic Route (camera); *Paint:* Plaid Enterprises; *Ink:* Ranger Industries; *Pen:* American Crafts; *Embroidery floss:* DMC; *Adhesive:* Scotch, 3M.

FINISH IT FASTER!
Skip stamping images and use premade elements.

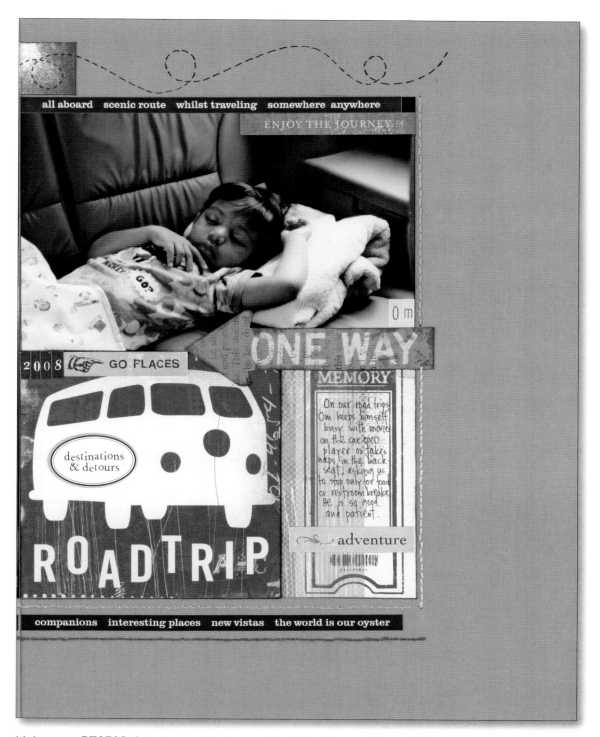

Make your **PHOTOS** the stars against a cardstock background by adding patterned-paper strips around them. For extra visual flair, stamp on portions, layer stickers and **STITCH** on photos and papers. Place your journaling on a stamped ticket.

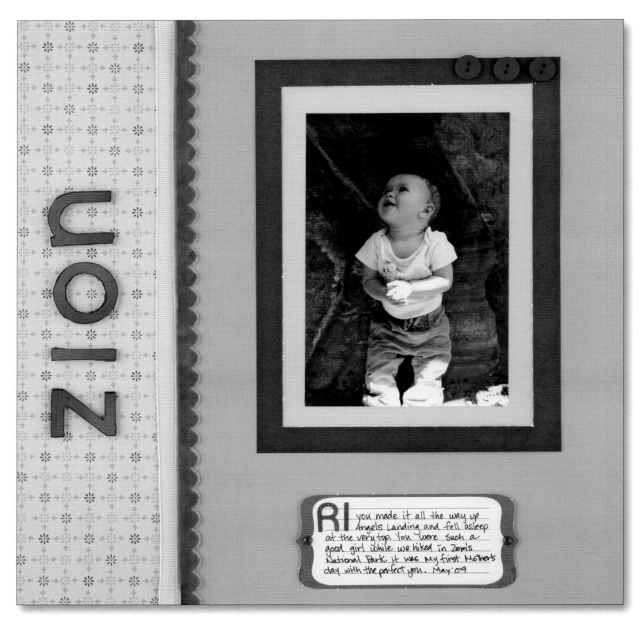

Zion | Kim Blackinton

Supplies *Cardstock and patterned paper:* Die Cuts With a View; *Tag:* My Mind's Eye; *Chipboard letters:* Chatterbox; *Ribbon:* Cosmo Cricket (yellow) and Making Memories (brown); *Buttons:* We R Memory Keepers; *Brads:* KI Memories; *Letter stickers:* BasicGrey; *Pen:* Newell Rubbermaid; *Adhesive:* Glue Dots International and Scrapbook Adhesives by 3L.
Bright idea: Dress up a paper "frame" with buttons.

Emphasize a great shot by **DOUBLE-MATTING** it on cardstock and patterned paper. Position the photo off-center on a sheet of background paper. Add patterned paper at left, **COVERING** the seam with ribbon. Cut, outline and attach a title.

FINISH IT FASTER!
Use title letters as is and skip the outlining.

Rockin' Around the Christmas Tree | Kelly Purkey

Supplies *Cardstock, patterned paper, buttons and pen:* American Crafts; *Stamps and rhinestones:* Hero Arts; *Ink:* StazOn, Tsukineko; *Die-cut machine:* Making Memories; *Adhesive:* Fiskars Americas; *Other:* Thread. **Bright idea:** Back a busy paper design with a neutral color to simplify the look.

FINISH IT FASTER!
Elevate and decorate die cuts with foam dots and buttons.

Keep your holiday memories **ALIVE** with a festive layout like this one! Trim patterned paper and mat it on background cardstock before adding your photo. Cut snowflakes with a **DIE-CUTTING** machine and adhere them to the page. Stamp a title onto strips, trim and adhere to page. Add journaling strips, buttons and rhinestones.

Garden Fresh | Lisa Swift

Supplies *Cardstock:* Die Cuts With a View; *Patterned paper:* Fancy Pants Designs (numbers) and Cosmo Cricket (all others); *Stickers:* KI Memories (epoxy) and Making Memories (letter and heart); *Chipboard:* Scenic Route and Sweetwater; *Journaling card:* My Mind's Eye; *Rub-ons:* Anna Griffin, Bo-Bunny Press, Doodlebug Design, Heidi Grace Designs, Heidi Swapp for Advantus and Sweetwater; *Ribbon:* May Arts; *Brads:* Bazzill Basics Paper and Doodlebug Design; *Adhesive:* Glue Dots International and Henkel Corporation; *Other:* Charm, tag and thread. **Bright idea:** Use numbered paper to suggest a produce growth chart.

FINISH IT FASTER!

For the most uniform circle, trace around a large lid or plate.

Perk up your **ALBUMS** with clever layout topics, but keep the process simple. Cut red patterned paper into a circle and adhere it to a cardstock background. Layer other papers over the **CIRCLE**, using text paper to mat the photos. Add embellishments, overlapping some over the photos.

Fond | Mou Saha

Supplies *Cardstock:* Die Cuts With a View; *Stickers:* American Crafts (title) and Making Memories (mini letters and number); *Rub-on:* BasicGrey; *Stamp:* Autumn Leaves; *Ink:* Tsukineko; *Sequins:* Darice; *Embroidery floss:* DMC; *Pen:* Newell Rubbermaid; *Font:* American Typewriter; *Adhesive:* Scotch, 3M. **Bright idea:** When adding bling to heritage pages, go tone on tone (purple here) to avoid over-powering the photo.

FINISH IT FASTER!

Draw elements extending onto your background paper rather than stitching.

Center a **TREASURED** photo vertically on cardstock, then stamp a design above. Pencil in extensions of the photo, then embroider the lines. Apply a rub-on below the photo and **EMBROIDER** portions. Add a sequin border along some photo edges for a subtle touch of shine.

Drawing | Kim Arnold

Supplies *Patterned paper, chipboard, stickers and ribbon:* Love, Elsie for KI Memories; *Transparency:* Hambly Screen Prints; *Paint:* Making Memories; *Adhesive:* Xpress IT; *Other:* Paper clips and pen. **Bright idea:** After painting chipboard letters black and letting them dry, coat them with Dimensional Magic for a glossy finish.

FINISH IT FASTER!
Use pre-colored chipboard letters instead of painting your own.

Anchor your photos with a cool border treatment. Tear an 11 ½" x 4" strip of patterned **PAPER** and cut a complementary ¾" x 11 ½" strip. Trim a piece of ledger paper to 3 ½" x 4 ¼". Position the paper strips as shown on top of a transparency, then attach **ANGLED** photos. Add a title (select a cute sticker to use as part of it!), journal and embellish.

Nature Study | Mou Saha

Supplies *Cardstock:* Die Cuts With a View; *Stickers:* Prima; *Ink:* Tsukineko; *Embroidery floss:* DMC; *Pen:* American Crafts; *Adhesive:* Scotch, 3M. **Bright idea:** Outline letter stickers with black pen to help them pop off the page.

FINISH IT FASTER!
Use dimensional paint to draw extending elements.

To achieve this stunning look, attach your photo, then pencil in extending **ELEMENTS**, like the branches and sidewalk here. Embroider designs and extend lines for a **COMPLEMENTARY** journaling shape.

the proof is in the picture

When I tell people I was a naughty kid, they look at me as if I'm totally exaggerating! But I was a rotten little thing! My parents had a 'no smack' policy til I was 5 or 6, but I should've got some earlier.

Recently I found this evidence - WHO DOES THIS TO THEIR NANA!!

yes that is me!

brat

PHOTO: grandpa tom (as mickey!), me, anna & nana bet. c. 1987

Brat | Emilie Robinson

Supplies *Cardstock:* Bazzill Basics Paper; *Patterned paper:* Junkitz; *Letter stickers:* Doodlebug Design (white), Provo Craft (black) and SEI (pink); *Brads:* Bumblebee Crafts; *Corner-rounder punch:* Carl Mfg.; *Rounded square cutter:* Curvy Cutter, EK Success. **Bright idea:** Guide the eye to an important photo element with a strip of paper in a bright color, and highlight your element with a ring of brads.

FINISH IT FASTER!
Use a specialty cutter to pare down time.

Bold patterned papers work best when tempered with a **NEUTRAL** paper, like the kraft cardstock on this page. Cut three curved paper shapes and trim the center from one to use for a tab. Adhere design elements, then attach the photo after rounding its corners. Add **JOURNALING** and brads.

Yeehah | Heidi Sonboul

Supplies *Cardstock:* Bazzill Basics Paper; *Patterned paper:* American Crafts and Hambly Screen Prints; *Letter stickers:* American Crafts; *Watercolor paint:* Crayola; *Foam sheets:* Jo-Ann Stores; *Adhesive:* Scotch, 3M; *Other:* Candy-box cover and toy compass. **Bright ideas:** Save and use old ephemera (like the "Round Up" candy-box cover here), or take apart an old toy and use its parts (like the compass here).

FINISH IT FASTER!
Use premade embellishments rather than cutting your own shaped designs from paper.

Cut a piece of patterned paper to 10" x 6" and adhere it to brown cardstock. Layer a **RIPPED** piece of white cardstock on top of the patterned paper. Add photos (rough up the sides a little to match the theme), letter stickers, a journaling tag and embellishments. **PAINT** "grass" by hand with watercolors.

Riley | Kim Blackinton

Supplies *Cardstock and chipboard embellishment:* Die Cuts With a View; *Patterned paper:* Colorbök; *Butterfly, quote, ribbon and chipboard letters:* Cosmo Cricket; *Brads and felt letters:* KI Memories; *Pen:* Newell Rubbermaid; *Adhesive:* Glue Dots International and Scrapbook Adhesives by 3L.

Spots of bright color really perk up this page. To get the look yourself, cut a **CIRCLE**, then adhere it to the back of a vertical photo. Position a horizontal photo next to it. Add patterned-paper strips and ribbon, then **ADORN** and include playful butterfly and flower accents.

FINISH IT FASTER!
Polish your page look with brads.

The Monsters Within | Suzy Plantamura

Supplies *Cardstock:* Bazzill Basics Paper; *Patterned paper, brackets, journaling tags and stickers:* October Afternoon; *Decorative scissors:* Fiskars Americas; *Adhesive:* EK Success; *Other:* Thread.

Create one circle from cardstock and a smaller version from patterned paper, then layer and add **STICKERS** for a quick title block. Include as many journaling blocks as needed—two work well here. Overlap patterned papers, using decorative-edged scissors on two edges. To reinforce the **"WACKY"** theme, stitch funky patterns with a sewing machine.

FINISH IT FASTER!

Draw random, messy "stitches" with a pen.

It's All Worth It | Joannie McBride

Supplies *Cardstock:* Prism Paper and The Paper Company; *Transparency:* Hambly Screen Prints; *Journaling spot:* Fancy Pants Designs; *Star die cut:* My Mind's Eye; *Chipboard phrases:* Chatterbox; *Rub-on letters and brads:* American Crafts; *Ribbon:* Close To My Heart; *Rhinestones:* KitoftheMonth.com; *Adhesive:* All Night Media and Fiskars Americas.

Position a piece of transparency carefully over cardstock and adhere with brads. Add photos, **SCALLOPED** cardstock and a journaling spot. Rise to elegant new heights with **RHINESTONES**, a raised star and journaling.

FINISH IT FASTER!
Wrap a star with ribbon for right-now flair.

For Sophie's third birthday, we went to Disneyland. We told her she could pick out one

THREE

3.
9.30.02

gift. She picked out this princess back pack and wore it all day while holding dadda's hand.

Three | Suzy Plantamura

Supplies *Patterned paper:* Bella Blvd. (blue), KI Memories (black, striped) and My Little Shoebox (pink); *Stickers:* Doodlebug Design; *Circle tag:* My Little Shoebox; *Rhinestone flower; Chipboard heart and rhinestones:* me & my BIG ideas; *Ribbon:* SEI; *Buttons:* Buttons Galore; *Border punch:* Fiskars Americas; *Pens:* EK Success (pink) and Sakura (white and black); *Adhesive:* EK Success and Glue Dots International. **Bright ideas:** Write journaling in white pen, and add "shadows" behind the letters with colored ink to help the writing stand out.

Border punches and **PREMADE** border stickers can bring decorative punch to your page in no time flat. Cut strips of paper for the background, layering some horizontally and some vertically. Use a border punch on two sides of one paper strip. Next, add border stickers to the edges of some paper strips. Cluster a group of **EMBELLISHMENTS** over the photos. Finish up with letter stickers, journaling, ribbon and buttons.

FINISH IT FASTER!

Use predesigned border strips or ribbon.

Bathing Beauty | Kathi Kirkland

Supplies *Cardstock:* Bazzill Basics Paper; *Patterned paper:* Graphic 45 and Making Memories; *Die cuts:* Graphic 45; *Chipboard letters and edge distresser:* Heidi Swapp for Advantus; *Rub-ons:* October Afternoon; *Letter stickers:* Making Memories; *Corner-rounder punch:* EK Success; *Ink:* Clearsnap; *Adhesive:* Scotch ATG, 3M; Fabri-Tac, Beacon Adhesives. **Bright idea:** Use ticket stubs or other ephemera to fit your theme or subject.

FINISH IT FASTER!
Use die-cut border strips instead of patterned-paper strips.

Scan and restore **VINTAGE** photos and select complementary patterned papers. (The narrower strips can be leftovers from your stash.) Layer the papers, overlap two photos, and lend an **ANTIQUE** feel with rub-ons and distressed edges.

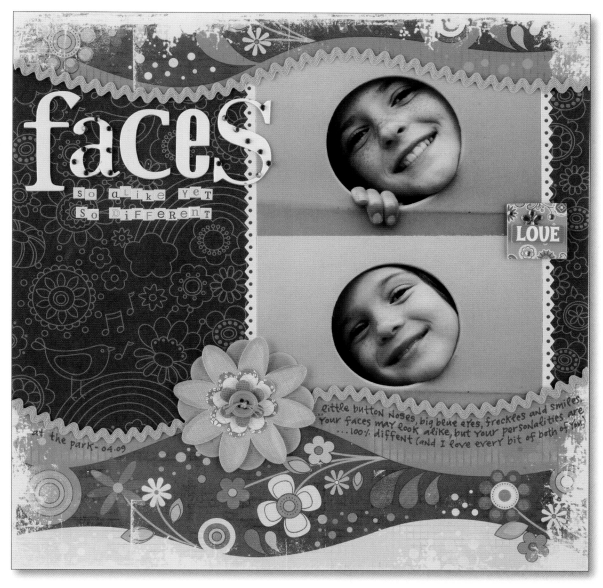

Faces | Suzy Plantamura

Supplies *Patterned paper:* My Little Shoebox (pink) and We R Memory Keepers (swirls and flowers); *Chipboard letters:* Prima and Heidi Swapp for Advantus; *Rhinestones and "Love" embellishment:* me & my BIG ideas; *Ledger letter stickers:* Adornit - Carolee's Creations; *Flowers:* Sassafras; *Embroidery floss:* DMC; *Pen:* Sharpie, Newell Rubbermaid; *Adhesive:* Duncan Enterprises, EK Success and Glue Dots International; *Other:* Rickrack and button. **Bright idea:** Short on title letters and need to mix a set? Add same-colored rhinestones or brads to help unify the look.

FINISH IT FASTER!
Spice up your border edge with "zigzag" scissors.

Balance the straight **ANGLES** of your photos with shapely accents. Select monochromatic paper for the background, then cut curved designs out of patterned paper. Add two horizontal photos at right, and place the **CURVED** designs so they overlap the photos. Embellish edges with rickrack. Use chipboard letters for a title, then journal by hand.

Laughing with Erin | Kelly Purkey

Supplies *Cardstock:* American Crafts (blue, red, yellow and white) and Bazzill Basics Paper (kraft); *Patterned paper:* Cosmo Cricket; *Specialty paper, ribbon and pen:* American Crafts; *Letter stickers:* BasicGrey; *Star, word bubble, border punches and adhesive:* Fiskars Americas; *Stamps:* Hero Arts; *Ink:* Memories, Stewart Superior Corporation; *Other:* Thread. **Bright idea:** Spread out a fun title on punched circles!

FINISH IT FASTER!

No stars on hand? Punch your own from specialty paper.

Attach patterned paper and **KRAFT** cardstock to white cardstock and trim. Mat on red cardstock. Punch blue cardstock with a border punch and adhere, then stitch to page. Fasten photo, ribbon and punched **YELLOW** cardstock to layout, and bring some spice to your journaling by adding it to a word bubble.

Backyard Popcorn | Vivian Masket

Supplies *Cardstock:* Bazzill Basics Paper; *Letter stickers:* American Crafts (red) and Making Memories (black and white); *Vinyl stickers and pen:* American Crafts; *Adhesive:* Kokuyo. **Bright idea:** Alter the same look for other layouts. Use a different corner design, stick with one or more photos, and flip the placement of the photos and text.

FINISH IT FASTER!
Whittle down design time with neutrals like white, black or kraft.

TEAR the right-hand edge of a landscape piece of 8 ½" x 11" cardstock, then adhere two photos at left. Add a title and journaling, and attach to a cardstock background. Frame the center block with **DECORATIVE** flourishes at top left and bottom right. So simple!

Beachy Ice Cream Bliss | Vivian Masket

Supplies *Cardstock:* Bazzill Basics Paper; *Patterned paper:* Scenic Route; *Letters and pen:* American Crafts; *Butterfly clip:* KI Memories; *Circle sticker:* 7gypsies; *Adhesive:* Kokuyo; *Other:* Staples. **Bright idea:** Interrupt your title with a fun embellishment between two words.

Snag this ultra-easy **DESIGN** for a super-fast finish. Cut two 4" x 6" pieces from patterned paper and tear one long side of each. Adhere the blocks (torn edges facing outward) with two photos between them. Use the left-hand block for design elements, and the right-hand block for **JOURNALING**.

FINISH IT FASTER!

Handwrite on grid patterned paper to make straight journaling a cinch.

Follow Your Dreams | Laina Lamb

Supplies *Cardstock:* Archiver's; *Patterned paper:* Collage Press; *Letter stickers:* American Crafts and Collage Press; *Stickers:* Jenni Bowlin Studio (ruler) and Making Memories (pebbles); *Chipboard:* Heidi Swapp for Advantus and me & my BIG ideas; *Star punch:* Stampin' Up!; *Page pebbles:* The Robin's Nest; *Rhinestones:* Mark Richards; *Staples:* Making Memories; *Adhesive:* 3M; *Other:* Thread and vintage typewriter. **Bright idea:** Type journaling on an antique typewriter for a faded, distressed look.

FINISH IT FASTER!
No sewing machine? Draw a thin line around the page for a frame.

Jumpstart your page design (and get more **MILEAGE** from scraps!) by layering patterned-paper pieces on cardstock. Add a photo, then machine-stitch on top of the picture and paper to create a frame. **JAZZ** up the layout with rhinestones, punches or other fun items.

Having Fun | Mou Saha

Supplies *Cardstock:* Die Cuts With a View; *Patterned paper:* Anna Griffin (orange-red) and Piggy Tales (blue and wheels); *Sticker:* Piggy Tales; *Ink:* Ranger Industries; *Circle punches:* Marvy Uchida; *Embroidery floss:* DMC; *Pen:* American Crafts; *Adhesive:* Scotch, 3M. **Bright idea:** Write journaling on a solid-colored background so it's readable against a busy background.

FINISH IT FASTER!

Forgo the hand-cut word.

High-energy photos deserve a high-energy design. **TRIM** patterned papers slightly smaller than the background cardstock and attach them. Mat the photos in a contrasting color, then center them on each side of the spread. **CLUSTER** embellishments and elevate them with foam tape. Hand-cut part of the title and spell out the rest with letter stickers. Add journaling strips and stitching.

Flower Girl | Brigid Gonzalez

Supplies *Software:* Adobe Photoshop CS3; *Digital papers and flower:* Vintage Florals by Shabby Princess; *Fonts:* Latin Modern Roman and Porcelain. **Bright ideas:** Use Adobe Photoshop's Eraser tool to remove an unwanted portion of a digital embellishment (a rickrack stem in this instance). Cut leftover paper scraps into sets of 6" x 6" and 4" x 4" pieces—they'll be ready for more pages with this versatile design!

FINISH IT FASTER!
Pre-cut paper triangles for speedy flowers anytime.

Combine your title and journaling to free up space for a **SNAZZY** decorative element. Choose two 4" x 6" photos, one horizontal and one vertical. Type your title and journaling on a 6" x 6" square of paper, then place a paper-pieced flower embellishment on a 4" x 4" square of the same paper. **ASSEMBLE** the layout on a 12" x 12" sheet of patterned paper, placing the photos at right angles to each other and leaving a 1" margin on all sides.

Compliment | lisa dickinson

Supplies *Cardstock:* Bazzill Basics Paper; *Patterned paper:* BasicGrey; *Chipboard letters, photo corners and file tab:* Heidi Swapp for Advantus; *Journaling sheet:* Knock, Knock, *www.knockknock.biz; Chipboard letters:* Maya Road; *Lined stamp:* FontWerks; *Brad:* Making Memories; *Pen:* American Crafts.

Fun in the Sun | Lori Anderson

Supplies *Cardstock:* Die Cuts With a View; *Patterned paper:* October Afternoon (floral) and Scenic Route (orange sunburst and yellow dot); *Chipboard:* Jenni Bowlin Studio (sun) and Sandylion (others); *Rub-on:* Little Yellow Bicycle; *Cork scallop strip:* Chatterbox; *Paint:* Making Memories; *Letter stickers and pen:* American Crafts; *Font:* CK Soccer Mom; *Adhesive:* Therm O Web and Tombow; *Other:* Rickrack and thread. **Bright idea:** Print a draft of your journaling block and trace the overlapping accent on top to see where the text needs to wrap.

FINISH IT FASTER!
Let the sewing machine rest and use rub-on stitches instead.

Blocking your photos with patterned paper makes for an easily assembled design! Cut a 4″ x 4″ and a 6″ x 6″ block of patterned paper. **ADHERE** the blocks alongside the photos to make a square on cardstock. Machine-stitch along the interior edges. Add **RICKRACK** and a cork scallop strip. Brighten the page with a chipboard sun, rub-ons and letter stickers.

too CUTE

BUNNY

springtime

hoppy easter

emmitt you are such a little cutie pie! You have such a Great imagination and love to MAKE-Believe. You had so much fun hiding the eggs and pretending to be the Bunny!
-february 2008

Too Cute | Laina Lamb

Supplies *Cardstock:* Bazzill Basics Paper; *Patterned paper:* Making Memories; *Stickers:* American Crafts (letter) and Making Memories (other); *Buttons:* Autumn Leaves; *Letter die cuts:* QuicKutz; *Circle punch:* EK Success; *Pen:* Uni-ball Signo, Newell Rubbermaid; *Adhesive:* 3M and All Night Media. **Bright idea:** To change up a square sticker, punch it into a circle shape and mat it with a white circle.

FINISH IT FASTER!
Fake stitches on buttons with a white pen.

Run a horizontal paper strip across a page to visually "ground" design elements. Next, mat a **FAVORITE** photo and tear the edges on one side for artistic flair. Journal right on the dark background cardstock with a white pen. Top off the page with **BUTTONS** and stickers.

Horizon | susan opel

Supplies *Cardstock:* Bazzill Basics Paper and Prima; *Patterned paper, rub-ons, cardstock stickers and gel embellishment:* KI Memories; *Flower:* Doodlebug Design; *Brown letters:* Chatterbox; *Font:* AL Uncle Charles, downloaded from *www.twopeasinabucket.com*.

Use *strips* of cardstock and patterned paper to lead the viewer's eye to a special photograph.

"My daughter and I *love* this fun summer activity: We wander around our hometown and photograph items that start with the letters A–Z. At the end of our field trip, we order prints. When the *prints* arrive, we put each 4" x 6" print on a 6" x 6" page, which gives us just enough room to add a letter sticker and a sentence or two of journaling."

—RACHEL THOMAE

right now
we are here
and nothing can mar
our perfection,
or steal the joy
of this perfect

MoMent

FEB 07 2008

Perfect Moment | lisa dickinson

Supplies *Patterned paper:* Ever After Scrapbook Co. (yellow); *Flower stickers:* Pebbles Inc.; *Chipboard letters and photo corner:* Heidi Swapp for Advantus; *Ribbon:* C.M. Offray & Son; *Brads:* Bazzill Basics Paper; *Ink:* ColorBox, Clearsnap; *Pen:* Pigma Micron, Sakura; *Font:* Diesel, downloaded from *www.urbanfonts.com*; *Other:* Red patterned paper, staples and date stamp.

Everyday Moments | lisa tilmon

Supplies *Cardstock:* Bazzill Basics Paper; *Patterned paper, ribbon and chipboard title accent:* We R Memory Keepers; *Rub-ons:* Mustard Moon; *Pen:* Stampin' Up!.

Crop your

photograph

to fit in a geometric

design on your page.

Pair cropped *photos* with patterned-paper strips to create a page design that flows.

Little Miss Manipulator | amber ries

Supplies *Software:* Photoshop CS2, Adobe Systems; *Digital paper and ribbons:* Streetwear by Tracy Robinson, www.scrapbook-bytes.com; *Digital clock embellishment and word tab:* Katie Pertiet, www.designerdigitals.com; *Digital typewriter keys:* Jenna Robertson, www.scrapmonkey.com; *Digital sewing stitches:* Nancie Rowe-Janitz, www.scrapartist.com; *Fonts:* SleepTalk, 1942 Report, Paulinho Pedra Azul and Reservoir, downloaded from the Internet.

Bubbles | sara dickey

Supplies *Cardstock:* Bazzill Basics Paper; *Patterned paper, ribbon and chip-board:* We R Memory Keepers; *Rub-ons:* Mustard Moon; *Pen:* Stampin' Up!.

"Remember a long time ago when I was in black and white?" asked Scarlett. "Remember back when you were the little girl and I was the mommy?"

I quickly realized that Scarlett could not conceive of a time before she was born. She didn't understand what it meant not to exist. I tried to explain the concept to her a few times but she just couldn't grasp it. Actually, I find her viewpoint quite fascinating...

Conversations with Scarlett, three years old, Winter 2005.

Black & White | lisa moorefield
Supplies *Cardstock:* Bazzill Basics Paper; *Letter stickers and ribbon:* Making Memories; *Fonts:* Franklin Gothic Medium and Times New Roman, Microsoft.

Group two 4" x 6" photos where *both sides* of a two-page layout meet.

"With *digital* photos, file size is everything, so I always make sure to use a memory stick with at least one gigabyte of *memory* (or you can keep an extra memory stick in your camera bag). This way, I can take higher-resolution images so when I crop in on a photo, I don't lose sharpness. Then, I can print out that great cropped *image* as a full 4" x 6" photo!"

—LORI FAIRBANKS

Angel, I just can't explain how much I love you. Since the day Daddy and I brought you and Daniel home, my world has been complete. I never could have imagined that I would have a little girl as perfect as you. Nor could I have ever imagined that you would be just like me. To me this is proof that a bond between a mother and daughter is made up of more than blood alone... it takes love.

Love | michelle tornay

Supplies *Cardstock:* Bazzill Basics Paper; *Patterned paper and chipboard letters:* Scenic Route; *Chipboard heart:* Heidi Swapp for Advantus; *Paint:* Delta Creative; *Pen:* Sakura.

Have *two* similar poses that you love? Group your two 4" x 6" photos in the center of your layout and offset them slightly.

photo keepsake box

Because my husband and I live so far away from our families, I love to give and receive photo gifts and photo cards. Since cards are often tucked away by their recipients, I wanted to create a gift that is both memorable and functional. The solution? A photo keepsake box. I decorated a plain chipboard cigar box—I used the Plain Jane cigar box by Cosmo Cricket—and slipped a 4" x 6" print behind the frame. It took me less than 15 minutes to complete. Here's how:

1. Adhere patterned paper to the sides and cover of the box. *Note:* Before adhering the bottom strip on the cover, add a small strip of ribbon as a tab to open the box.

2. Embellish the cover with a rub-on or sticker.

3. Adhere patterned paper inside the box.

4. Add a photo behind the frame cutout. (I used photo corners to hold my photo in place, making it easy for the recipient to switch out photos. I also used two photos back to back so I could display a photo on the inside as well.)

Variation: This project is fast and super-easy to adapt by simply using different patterned papers. I made two more gift boxes the next night for my mother and sister by choosing different floral prints and adding ribbon for a feminine touch!

—by vanessa hoy

Happy Anniversary | vanessa hoy

Supplies *Chipboard cigar box:* Cosmo Cricket; *Patterned paper:* Die Cuts With a View; *Rub-on phrase and doodle:* Déjà Views, The C-Thru Ruler Co.; *Ribbon brad:* Karen Foster Design.

MAXIMIZE YOUR 4" X 6" PHOTOS

Help your photos shine with these quick tricks

Want to add more "oomph" to photos as you scrapbook them? You can! Simply pinpoint nonessential areas within your pictures (such as bland or blurry backdrops) and cover them. That's right—you're not stuck with a so-so area just because it was part of the original shot Instead, tweak the static space with quick, easy additions. Here's how.

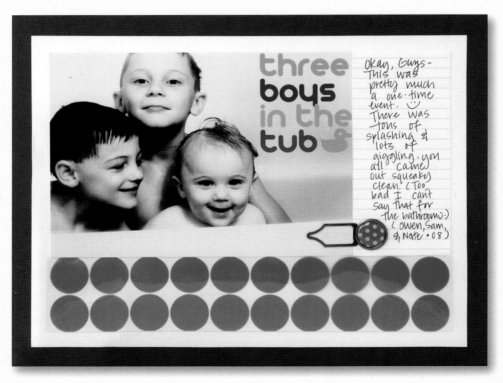

Three Boys in the Tub | Candice Palmer

Supplies *Patterned paper:* October Afternoon; *Clip:* Making Memories; *Transparency:* Hambly Screen Prints; *Fonts:* Arista and Efon; *Other:* Pen.

① Add a title or journaling.

After testing first on scratch paper, write directly on the photo with a safe, non-smear pen. A white pen works beautifully against dark backgrounds. Or, as a goof-proof alternative, add text digitally. You can include your own handwriting with a pen tablet or choose from thousands of fonts online. Another popular solution? Apply rub-on phrases, letters or words. You get journalistic and decorative flair in seconds!

Kurt first learned to play the guitar for the usual reasons—to join a band and attract chicks. Now he leads a music team in his church. He's rockin' out for God these days!

Guitar Guy | Beth Opel

Supplies *Patterned paper:* Bo-Bunny Press (dot) and Jenni Bowlin Studio (shaped); *Letter stickers:* American Crafts (black) and Close To My Heart (white); *Brads:* Making Memories; *Font:* CK Jot; *Adhesive:* Click 'n Stick Mounting Squares by Scrapbook Adhesives, 3L.

SWITCH IT UP!

Sure, you can stick with basic arrangements, but why not shake things up a bit? Following are three quick suggestions from 2008 *Creating Keepsakes* Hall of Fame member Linda Rodriguez:

- Add dimension with foam dots. Leave some photos and elements flat while "lifting" others.

- Place chipboard letters across a cluster of photographs. Adhere four photos, corner to corner, then add a title of chipboard letters that spans across the top of two photos and across the bottom of two photos. This works especially well when you have several photos on the page and little room for a title.

- Line up photos across a page to show a chronological succession. For a fun twist, stagger the photos from the bottom-left corner to the upper-right corner (ascending or descending).

From This Day Forward | Beth Opel

Supplies *Cardstock:* WorldWin; *Patterned paper:* Doodlebug
Design (blue glitter) and SEI (yellow floral); *Letter stickers:*
American Crafts (black) and Pink Paislee (blue); *Paper border:*
Doodlebug Design; *Acrylic rub-on and chipboard:* American
Crafts; *Punches:* Marvy Uchida (round scalloped) and Martha
Stewart Crafts (scalloped border); *Adhesive:* Click 'n Stick
Mounting Squares by Scrapbook Adhesives, 3L; Zip Dry Paper
Glue, Beacon Adhesives; *Other:* Pen and rhinestones.

(2) Embellish to draw the eye.

Take "blah" photo areas from dull to
dazzling by adding flowers, buttons,
charms and more. Limit the number to
avoid visual complexity, and choose
style, color and size with care. (Place
each item on the layout to see how it
works with the photos. Notice what
draws your eye and is complementary
to the photos and the page.)

Photo | Sara Winnick
Supplies *Other:* Butterfly stamp, cardstock, ink and glitter.

10 TRICKS FOR BETTER-LOOKING LAYOUTS

You've learned to maximize the space within your photos—now's the perfect time to streamline their arrangement. Here's how to get the best results in record time with ease:

1. Follow a template or sketch. You won't need to figure out design basics, since someone else has done the initial work for you. Choose a look you already love and get right to sizing and placing photos. As you scrapbook, tinker as needed to make the results work for you. For sketches using 4"x 6" photos, turn to pg. 242.

2. Mat your photos digitally. When printing your pictures, leave a ⅛" to ¼" white border around each to create an instant photo mat.

3. Crop multiple photos at a time. Line them up side by side on a large trimmer. Cut in a single pass on each side. You'll get more exact measurements and shave off precious minutes.

4. Use a ruler and pencil to lightly mark precise photo positions. Eliminate guesswork by measuring and marking before you adhere anything. If desired, create a temporary visual "guideline" with string or a laser level (available at home-improvement stores).

5. Group digital images as a collage before printing. You can then readily place the collage on your page.

6. Adhere several photos tightly in a block on cardstock. Trim and attach the entire section to the background of your layout if desired for easier handling.

7. Cut a thin paper strip to use as a visual guide. You can place it between photos or other elements when you need to keep an equal distance between components on a page. (Of course, nothing *needs* to match up—it's perfectly okay to tilt page elements for visual variety.)

8. Don't be afraid to arrange photos with sides touching. Depending on the photos, you can often skip worrying about leaving "white space" between them. Or, create your own margins with pen or paint borders instead.

9. For the most aesthetic results, note where your photo subject is looking. Generally, the subject should be looking "into"—not away from—the layout.

10. Camouflage with flair. Do you need to disguise a distracting flaw? Cover the problem area with ribbon, a paper strip or your embellishment of choice.

britney mellen

from camera to composition

Here's a little expert advice from Britney on creating layouts with 4" x 6" photos. Follow her creative process in this Q & A to see how she puts a layout together.

Q What is the story behind these pictures?

A These were all taken at the Louvre in Paris. I was excited to scrapbook these photos—just look at the rich, regal colors, and at the beautiful artwork! I knew these photos would speak for themselves.

Q How did you choose the photos you used on this layout?

A I've always been taught that photos with people are the most interesting pictures, but I wanted the art to be the focus on this layout, so I selected photos of the architecture and artwork that was on display.

Outside the Louvre

On the way to the Louvre

Q How did you choose the colors and embellishments for your layout?

A I chose rich, jewel-toned colors for my papers to bring out the majestic quality of the photos. I wanted the embellishments to match the style of the photos, so I found intricate rub-ons that fit the mood. I drew attention to the Aphrodite statue by adding a ribbon photo corner in a texture and color that matched the page.

The Pyramid

The crowds

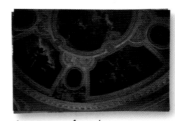

Amazing ceilings!

Venus de Milo

THE...

LOUVRE

What better way to spend Valentines Day other than Paris? And... Who better to pay a visit to on Valentines Day other than the one and only Aphrodite -- aka Venus de Milo, the Greek goddess of love? Seeing the famous statue was, to me, like meeting a celebrity -- a fascinating icon of art, religion and history.

February 2007

The Louvre | britney mellen

Supplies *Cardstock:* Bazzill Basics Paper; *Patterned paper:* Daisy D's Paper Co.; *Rub-ons:* Die Cuts With a View; *Ribbon:* SEI; *Pen:* American Crafts.

layouts with

3

photos

he

Wade Foust

always wore coveralls

was a ham radio operator

taught me how to spell my name in Morse code

kept Fruit Stripe gum in his desk

made lamps, digital clocks and other things

had the first computer I ever saw (late 1970s)

loved sweet potatoes

chewed tobacco

made hand-cranked ice cream

called Robbie "peanut butter boy"

died when I was ten years old

was my Grandpa

... and these are the things I remember most about him.

2007

He | lisa moorefield

Supplies *Cardstock:* Bazzill Basics Paper; *Mini brads:* Making Memories; *Font:* Times New Roman, Microsoft; *Other:* Thread.

How do you like these pictures? Do they look forced? No? Well, lucky me. Because, these all came from our second trip to the pumpkin patch in 2008. Why a second trip you ask? Because the 50+ pictures I took the first time disappeared from the memory card before we got home. I was devastated when I sat down to the computer and tried to download them. Then Quinn said, "Let's go again". So of course I say "What? Go again...just to take pictures" (he knows I love pumpkin patch pictures). "Yeah, why not" he says. Seriously? How sweet (and smart — I didn't think of it!) is that? The new pictures aren't nearly as good as the first — but the memories are better! Plus, we got to buy another dozen of the amazing homemade donuts they sell at the patch — score!

Pumpkin Patch | Jamie Kuhnhausen

Supplies *Cardstock:* Bazzill Basics Paper; *Patterned paper:* BasicGrey and Creative Imaginations; *Transparency:* Little Yellow Bicycle; *Buttons:* BasicGrey; *Rub-ons:* October Afternoon; *Stickers:* BasicGrey (brown) and Doodlebug Design; *Corner-rounder punch:* Creative Memories; *stamp:* 7gypsies; *Font:* Futura Lt; *Adhesive:* Therm O Web; *Other:* Buttons. **Bright idea:** This design is easily adapted for different orientations— for example, try using one portrait photo with two landscape photos.

Punch corners on each photo, then secure each to the background. **OVERLAP** two complementary pieces of paper and add a festive journaling block. If you have lots of journaling, like Jamie did, use a **TRANSPARENCY** on top to break up the text and reinforce your theme. Add a stamped circle, letters and buttons.

FINISH IT FASTER!
Cover the intersection between papers with buttons.

One Size Fits All | shannon taylor

Supplies *Metal-rimmed tag:* Making Memories; *Plastic letters:* Heidi Swapp for Advantus; *Letter stickers:* Reminisce, Arctic Frog and Mustard Moon; *Glaze:* Mod Podge, Plaid Enterprises; *Adhesive:* Super Tape, Therm O Web; *Font:* Yelly, downloaded from the Internet; *Other:* Cardstock, tissue paper and a corrugated box.

For a clean look, crop your *favorite* images to the same size and group them in one block on your page.

LAS VEGAS *nightlife*

I called Las Vegas home for three years. Now when I visit I reminisce about beautiful desert nights behind the wheel of my Grand Am cruising The Strip marveling at the lights and the vibrancy and the pulse of this amazing American destination. On those nights I was a Midwestern girl transported to a twinkling wonderland. There's just nothing like Las Vegas at night, baby!

Las Vegas | susan opel

Supplies *Cardstock:* Bazzill Basics Paper; *Ribbon, epoxy letters and stickers:* Creative Imaginations; *Brad:* KI Memories; *Gems:* Mark Jacobs; *Font:* Eurostar, Microsoft.

Sometimes I can't get a smile out of you, but I still take your picture.

All days deserve to be remembered.

Even those days when your friends were less than friendly ...

and your pony was being difficult.

Thankfully we don't have too many of those days.

Serious | maria gallardo-williams

Supplies *Cardstock:* Bazzill Basics Paper; *Patterned paper:* Imaginisce; *Die cuts:* Legacy Paper Arts; *Ink:* Memories, Stewart Superior Corporation; *Chipboard letters:* Chatterbox and Heidi Swapp for Advantus; *Letter stickers:* Chatterbox; *Flowers:* Prima; *Brads:* Queen & Co.; *Font:* Lucida Handwriting, Microsoft.

Give your layout a

layered

look by slightly overlapping your photos and frames.

Flip Flop | kim moreno

Supplies *Patterned paper:* Dream Street Papers; *Chipboard circle:* Everlasting Keepsakes; *Sticker and rub-on:* American Crafts; *Letter tabs:* Autumn Leaves; *Brads:* Making Memories; *Ink:* ColorBox Fluid Chalk, Clearsnap; *Pen:* Pigma Micron, Sakura.

Highlight the focus of

each photo

by placing a large circle on the group of photos.

Seriously | lisa truesdell

Supplies *Cardstock:* Bazzill Basics Paper; *Patterned paper:* Autumn Leaves (dark blue, tan) and KI Memories (light blue); *Buttons, brads, pen and ribbon:* American Crafts; *Label sticker:* 7gypsies; *Coaster circles:* Gin-X, Imagination Project; *Other:* Ledger paper.

"When working with *multiple* photos, I find it's much easier if I have one that stands out in some way—a close-up over action shots, a portrait-oriented picture mixed with landscapes, or a black-and-white *picture* to play off of some color shots. This gives me both a place to start my page design and a *focus* for my journaling and title."

—LISA TRUESDELL

Explore | jeri hoag

Supplies *Patterned paper, chipboard letters and stamps:* Fancy Pants Designs; *Ink:* Tsukineko; *Felt:* Foss Manufacturing Company.; *Pinking-edge scissors:* Hobby Lobby; *Font:* Times New Roman, Microsoft.

Keep the focus on your

focal-point

photo by cropping another photo
you don't want to draw
as much attention to.

Secrets | vivian masket
Supplies *Cardstock:* Bazzill Basics Paper; *Patterned paper, chipboard stars and pen:* American Crafts; *Journaling sticky note:* Heidi Swapp for Advantus.

Crop a *series* of three 4" x 6" photographs to 4" x 4". Set off the focal-point photo by adhering it to a strip of bold patterned paper and then layering it over the other two photographs.

"Scrapping 4" x 6" pictures is very *freeing*. Just take them out of the envelope from the photo lab and start scrapping . . . *no fussing* with sizes! I love that!"

—MARIA GALLARDO-WILLIAMS

Here's a story of a guy named Kelcey He met a girl named Julie and fell in love and then finally they got married And it was all pretty & lovely. That's how they became

the KINJO BUNCH

The Kinjo Bunch | caroline ikeji

Supplies *Cardstock:* Bazzill Basics Paper; *Patterned paper:* American Crafts and KI Memories; *Letter stickers:* Scrapworks and American Crafts; *Chipboard letters:* Heidi Swapp for Advantus; *Photo corners:* KI Memories; *Brads and pen:* American Crafts; *Other:* Lace.

Give your *layout* a twist by mixing black-and-white and color photos. Leave your focal-point photo in color and place it next to the title to draw attention to it.

Pose | tiffany tillman

Supplies *Software:* Adobe Photoshop 7.0, Adobe Systems; *Digital patterned papers and elements:* Cuddlebug Digital Kit by Shabby Princess, *www.theshabbyshoppe.com;* *Font:* Mom's Typewriter, downloaded from *www.dafont.com.*

Mat your focal-point photo on *patterned* paper to help it stand out from a photo grouping.

"For *portrait-oriented* photos, I love to use a design that lines my photos up side by side. It's a quick and effective way to design a page around a *series* of equal photos."

—BARBARA PFEFFER

Frosty Fun | barbara hogan

Supplies *Cardstock:* WorldWin, *Patterned paper:* Sassafras Lass; *Ink:* Stampin' Up!; ColorBox, Clearsnap; StazOn, Tsukineko; *Snowflake brads:* Making Memories; *Gems:* Westrim Crafts; *Ribbon:* May Arts; *Clear ring:* Junkitz; *Glitter paint:* Duncan Enterprises; *Pens:* Uni-ball Signo and Sharpie, Sanford.

Loved | lisa dickinson, photos by laurita fotographia

Supplies *Cardstock:* Bazzill Basics Paper; *Patterned paper:* BasicGrey; *Chipboard flowers:* Melissa Frances; *Letter stickers:* Chatterbox; *Ribbon:* May Arts; *Font:* Susie's Hand, downloaded from the Internet.

Idea to note: Lisa hand-cut the patterned-paper design to create an intricate border, perfect for this feminine page!

This is so typical you and so typical of your outdoor boy play. Why just run through the sprinkler, when you can drive a trike through it? Why stay on the trike, when you can fall off of it? And why be quiet when you can make all kinds of cool sound effects? That mischievous grin on your face says it all. Why have a little fun, when it can be all out good, clean, summer fun?!

good clean summer fun

Summer Fun | greta hammond

Supplies *Cardstock:* Bazzill Basics Paper; *Patterned paper and chipboard letters:* Scenic Route; *Rub-ons:* FontWerks and Scenic Route; *Letter stickers:* Making Memories; *Button:* Autumn Leaves; *Circle stamp:* FontWerks; *Font:* Times New Roman, Microsoft; *Other:* Ink.

Winter Bliss | amber tosh

Supplies *Cardstock:* Bazzill Basics Paper; *Patterned paper and cardstock stickers:* Melissa Frances; *Letter die cuts:* Cricut, Provo Craft; *Ink:* ColorBox, Clearsnap; *Pen:* Creative Memories; *Other:* Ribbon and button.

Draw the *eye* to your focal-point photo by mounting it on contrasting papers.

HiP HOP

see for yourself

I have to admit to having some misgivings when Jackie assigned you to the new hip-hop competition number. I really wasn't sure you could pull it off. Sure you're a good dancer and a willing learner. But hip-hop isn't just a style of dance, it's an entire culture. It's not just in the steps, but in the presentation. I didn't know if you had it in you, even after months of rehearsal. But once your costume arrived and you donned it, a transformation took place. Because when it comes to hip-hop, it's all about the attitude. And girl, I think you've got it!

Jm. 07

it's all about the attitude

Hip Hop | barbara pfeffer

Supplies *Cardstock:* Bazzill Basics Paper; *Patterned paper and chipboard:* Scenic Route; *Foam letters:* American Crafts; *Stickers:* American Crafts and EK Success; *Font:* 2Peas Magic Forest, downloaded from *www.twopeasinabucket.com*.

Take *pictures* at various distances to add variety to similar photographs.

Surfing USA | barbara pfeffer

Supplies *Cardstock:* Bazzill Basics Paper; *Patterned paper, letter stickers and ribbon:* Arctic Frog; *Chipboard letters:* Pressed Petals; *Die cuts:* Sizzix, Ellison; *Fonts:* 2Peas Jack Frost, downloaded from *www.twopeasinabucket.com*; Nina, Microsoft.

Nick looked positively adorable in his surfer guy outfit for this year's dance recital. When he got up on that stage, his face lit up with excitement. He had such a great time and was so cute. The crowd just loved him! And so do I.

Group *three* vertical photos at the top of a 12" x 12" layout.

11 18 06

Perfect babes

Who said I'd be most likely to eat my own young? Psfft.

What do people in high school really know anyways?

7 years ago I would probably have agreed, I wasn't very maternal.

I wasn't really into the self-less giving, well, really my list of flaws was long.

But then I met the love of my life, all of sudden I longed for a family.

Now one thing that hasn't changed is my "go for the gusto" attitude.

I take nothing lightly. I knew one or two just wouldn't do it,

and here we are with 3 perfect babes and plenty of room in our hearts for more!

Perfect Babes | courtney kelly

Supplies *Patterned paper:* Scenic Route; *Stamps, paint and metal clips:* Making Memories; *Felt flowers and brads:* American Crafts; *Font:* AL Messenger, downloaded from *www.twopeasinabucket.com.*

"I like that I can make quick, *easy mats* for 4" x 6" photos or just put them on the layout without *cropping* them at all. I get a page done a lot faster this way! For me, it requires less thinking than trying to work with larger photos."

—SARA WISE

Butterfly Kisses | Suzy Plantamura

Supplies *Patterned paper:* Doodlebug Design (black and yellow glittered) and Little Yellow Bicycle (yellow with border); *Chipboard title block:* Pink Paislee; *Stickers:* Doodlebug Design (border) and Making Memories (letter); *Flowers:* Creative Imaginations (green) and unknown (black); *Chipboard leaves:* KI Memories; *Felt butterflies:* Heidi Swapp for Advantus; *Glitter:* Stampendous!; *Dimensional adhesive:* Diamond Glaze, JudiKins; *Adhesive:* Duncan Enterprises, EK Success and Glue Dots International; *Other:* Rickrack. **Bright ideas:** To add razzmatazz to a title block, outline it with rickrack. Use a border sticker along all of your photos to give them a unified look.

FINISH IT FASTER!
Apply clear adhesive and glitter directly to the butterflies.

Go glam with **GLITTER** cardstock (two different versions) as a background. Add photos, a title block (use a journaling sheet behind as a border), an embellishment cluster, a border sticker and **RICKRACK**. Create a clever journaling path with rickrack. Tuck ledger stickers beneath, bent slightly, so the letters "fly" behind the butterfly.

Apple of Our Eyes | Mou Saha

Supplies *Cardstock:* Die Cuts With a View; *Patterned paper:* Luxe Designs; *Buttons and stickers:* Rusty Pickle; *Apple accent:* KI Memories; *Stamps:* Michaels; *Ink:* Tsukineko; *Embroidery floss:* DMC; *Pen:* American Crafts; *Adhesive:* 3M and Therm O Web. **Bright idea:** Lend a cozy "quilt" touch with subtle patterned-paper squares and a blanket stitch.

Embroidery floss adds a homey **COZINESS** to Mou's page. Attach photos to cardstock, then adhere coordinating blocks of patterned paper around the photos. Embroider around the photos with a **BLANKET** stitch. Create a quick title with letter stickers, then add journaling, stickers, stamped images and a button border.

FINISH IT FASTER!
Journaling on your photo makes use of the "extra" space on the image.

Chicago Bulls | Kelly Purkey

Supplies *Cardstock:* American Crafts (dark brown) and Bazzill Basics Paper (kraft); *Patterned paper:* American Crafts (red) and October Afternoon (blue and stripe); *Stickers and brads:* American Crafts; *Stamps:* Hero Arts; *Ink:* Memories, Stewart Superior Corporation; *Rub-ons:* American Crafts and Heidi Grace Designs; *Circle cutter, punches and adhesive:* Fiskars Americas; *Font:* 2Peas Typo. **Bright idea:** Smooth the visual transition from photos to striped paper by placing a punched cardstock border on top.

FINISH IT FASTER!

Outline around the stars with a black pen rather than mounting them on cardstock.

Steal this design for your own page topic—it doesn't need to be about **SPORTS**. Attach photos block-style to a piece of cardstock. Add patterned paper at top right and adhere. Cut circles and offset slightly before affixing to layout. **FINISH** with letter stickers, rub-ons, journaling and more patterned paper.

Take 36 | Chrys Rose

Supplies *Cardstock:* Bazzill Basics Paper; *Patterned paper:* 7gypsies, American Crafts and Daisy D's Paper Co.; *Chipboard, die cut and stickers:* Scenic Route; *Buttons:* Boxer Scrapbook Productions; *Ribbon and staples:* Making Memories. **Bright idea:** Use a decorative arrow to spotlight your title.

FINISH IT FASTER!
Pass on the buttons and ribbon to make this layout in a jiffy!

Sometimes the **OUTTAKES** from a family photo shoot are just as memorable as the final piece! Tear a long piece of patterned paper and position it vertically on cardstock. Adhere a rectangular piece on top and sew the edges with a zigzag stitch before lifting them for texture. Add photos, ribbon and **RANDOM** embellishments. Frame your favorite photo with a paper-covered chipboard circle.

Library @ Winter | Kim Arnold

Supplies *Patterned paper:* Autumn Leaves (snowflake), KI Memories (blue) and Scenic Route (green); *Chipboard and die cuts:* Scenic Route; *Letter stickers:* American Crafts; *Pins and sticker:* Heidi Grace Designs; *Paper border:* Doodlebug Design; *Ribbon:* 7gypsies; *Transparency:* Hambly Screen Prints; *Adhesive:* Xpress IT. **Bright idea:** Dots and circles give the feeling of snow and reinforce a winter theme.

Specialty paper gives your page instant **ZING**. Attach a 4" x 11 ¼" strip of red patterned paper at left, then add a 12" x 8 ½" piece of paper (torn on one side). Layer **SNOWFLAKE** die-cut paper on top (cutting off the excess), followed by a transparency. Add photos and embellish freely.

FINISH IT FASTER!
Don't have a snowflake embellishment?
Use a large circle instead.

Chloe loves to play outside in the yard. She is either on her scooter, riding her bike or playing jump rope. Taylor, Cameron, Sophie and Brooke usually join in the fun. And then there's Mayzie—She chases them all! 08.08

Outdoor Play Is So Much Fun | Suzy Plantamura

Supplies *Patterned paper:* Creative Imaginations (green) and Jenni Bowlin Studio (cream/pink); *Felt and small pink flower:* Creative Imaginations; *Stickers:* Adornit - Carolee's Creations (small letters), Doodlebug Design (letters) and Hambly Screen Prints (border); *Fabric flower:* Prima; *Button and staples:* Making Memories; *Clip:* Provo Craft; *Rub-ons:* KI Memories (word) and SEI (flower); *Pens:* EK Success; *Adhesive:* Duncan Enterprises, EK Success and Glue Dots International; *Other:* Large pink flower, staples and thread. **Bright idea:** Use rub-ons right on your photo to fill in the background.

FINISH IT FASTER!
Forget perfection—cut a scalloped border from felt freehand.

Feel free to overlap pictures to fit more on your page. Cut the top off a sheet of patterned paper, then add another paper **DESIGN** behind to make up the depth. Cover the intersecting section with a transparency sticker. Cut scalloped borders out of polka-dot felt and **STAPLE** to page above and below photos. Add embellishments and stitching, layering them for interest.

My Adorable Boys | Allison Davis

Supplies *Cardstock:* Bazzill Basics Paper; *Patterned paper, transparency and die cuts:* My Mind's Eye; *Circle punch:* EK Success; *Letter stickers:* American Crafts; *Chipboard:* Maya Road; *Felt embellishments:* Fancy Pants Designs; *Ink:* ColorBox Fluid Chalk, Clearsnap; *Spray ink:* Tattered Angels; *Embroidery floss:* DMC; *Adhesive:* All Night Media, Tombow and Scrapbook Adhesives by 3L. **Bright idea:** Laying out circles (or even hearts, stars or squares) from punched shapes is a great way to replicate patterned paper.

FINISH IT FASTER!
Stamp circles with a large circle stamp.

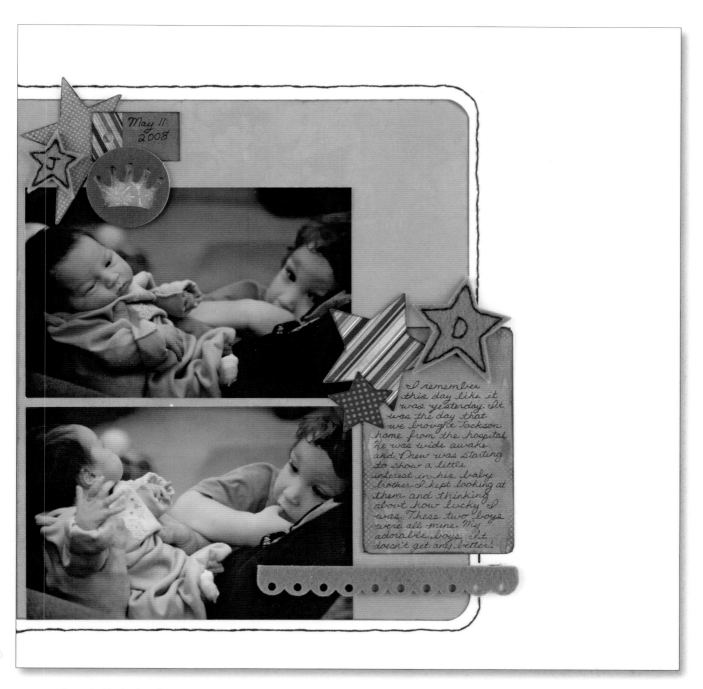

Punch 1" circles from a variety of patterned papers and ink the edges if desired. Adhere them in a **GRID** pattern on the left-hand page, working around the photo and title. Incorporate a solid-colored paper at right to help **BALANCE** the "busy" design at left. Add remaining photos, then place the embellishments and journaling card in a triangle around the pictures.

and i said

I never really saw myself as the mom type. I was never one of those people that gushed over babies or that made silly faces to make a tight lipped toddler smile. I was the person that darted out of the room when someone offered up opportunities to hold the baby. I also did my fair share of teeth grinding when I heard a toddler throwing a "fit in public. I might have even thrown out a few," I'm never having kids!" But I did have kids. I'm sure that all moms would agree with me when I say that having kids completely changes you. It changes you in the most wonderful and happy ways. Now I always rush to pick up my sweet baby Jackson and I never hesitate to smother his chubby cheeks with kisses. I never miss an opportunity to have a dance party with Drew and we can spend hours using our imagination to travel to outer space. Now I can't imagine life without my boys. And I thought I wasn't the mom type!

Love you   I love you   I love you   I love you   I lov

LOVE

And I Said I Wasn't the Mom Type | Allison Davis

Supplies *Cardstock:* Bazzill Basics Paper; *Patterned paper, chipboard letters and chipboard embellishments:* Fancy Pants Designs; *Letter stickers:* Making Memories; *Ink:* ColorBox Fluid Chalk, Clearsnap; *Paint:* Making Memories; *Pen:* Zig Writer, EK Success; *Adhesive:* Glue Dots International and Scrapbook Adhesives by 3L. **Bright idea:** Trace around an element and place your journaling over the design. Write outside the design with a black pen and inside the element in a different color.

FINISH IT FASTER!
Find an existing curved-edge strip on patterned paper, cut it out and adhere.

Create fabulous **FLOW** with a wavy paper strip, rounded photo block and swirly chipboard shape. (Check out the fun patterned paper behind.) Add photos and accents. Draw lines and add journaling with a pencil and a ruler; **TRACE** a heart over it, then write journaling in different colors and erase all the pencil lines.

Horseback Ride | Ria M. Mojica

Supplies *Cardstock:* Provo Craft; *Patterned paper:* Jenni Bowlin Studio (blue damask) and Sassafras (rainbows and clouds); *Chipboard:* American Crafts (letters) and Chatterbox (others); *Ink:* Clearsnap; *Pen:* American Crafts; *Adhesive:* 3M. **Bright ideas:** Punch a square in patterned paper and overlay it atop your 4" x 6" photo. No cropping required.

Create energy by setting your design on an **ANGLE**. Arrange photos, paper blocks and journaling in three columns, then tilt and position the 11" x 11" page on a larger, solid background. **FINISH** the page by adding a title and embellishments.

FINISH IT FASTER!
Frame a small photo for extra emphasis.

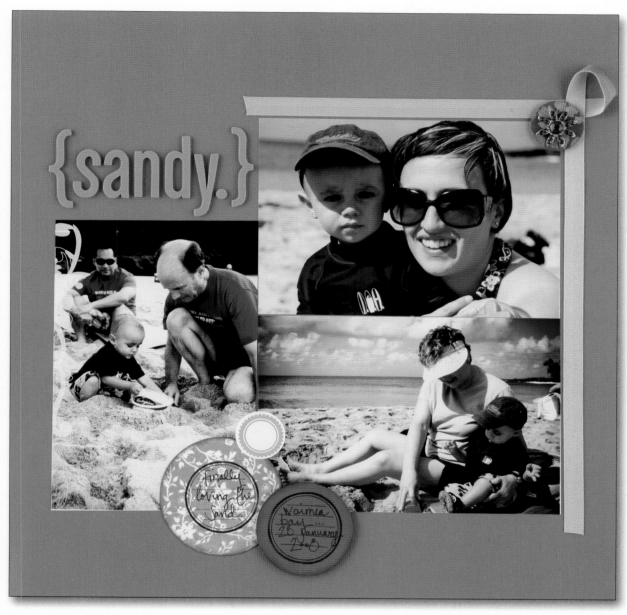

Sandy | Katie Anaya

Supplies *Cardstock:* Bazzill Basics Paper; *Patterned paper:* BasicGrey and Cross-My-Heart; *Rub-on:* BasicGrey; *Chipboard and circle sticker:* Scenic Route; *Letter stickers and ribbon:* American Crafts; *Stamp:* 7gypsies; *Other:* Ink.

Showcase three **FAVORITE** photos in a grouping, dressed up with stamps, ribbon, stickers and rub-ons. Set the title off **STYLISHLY** in brackets.

FINISH IT FASTER!

Loop and adorn ribbon for a fancy photo frame.

You Are Mine | Wendy Kwok

Supplies *Cardstock:* Bazzill Basics Paper; *Patterned paper:* October Afternoon and Pink Paislee; *Stickers:* American Crafts (puffy) and Pink Paislee (other); *Chipboard cupcake:* Maya Road; *Paint:* Making Memories; *Scallop punch:* Fiskars Americas; *Other:* Glitter. **Bright idea:** Use a dash of bright color to draw attention to the main photo.

Punch and layer patterned papers on cardstock, add a **TRIANGULAR** title block, then place three photos side by side on top. Don't worry if a photo is slightly blurry—that's okay. **SWEETEN** the page with a chipboard cupcake (decorated with paint and glitter) and add journaling.

FINISH IT FASTER!

"Point" to your favorite items with a patterned-paper triangle.

Our Soccer Champ | Laina Lamb

Supplies *Cardstock:* Bazzill Basics Paper; *Patterned paper:* Dream Street Papers; *Journaling spot:* Heidi Swapp for Advantus and Maya Road; *Letter stickers:* American Crafts; *Rub-ons:* Doodlebug Design; *Corner-rounder punch:* EK Success; *Star brad and epoxy shape:* Making Memories; *Adhesive:* 3M and All Night Media.

For a switch, go **VERTICAL** when adding titles, accents or photo groupings to a page background. Use a corner-rounder punch (with the guard off) to create a **SCALLOP** strip.

FINISH IT FASTER!
Punch a photo into a circle and mat it in a pinch.

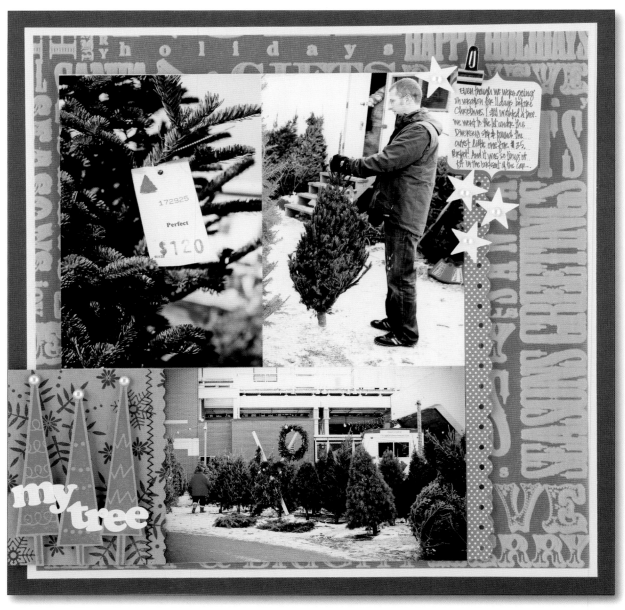

My Tree | Kelly Purkey

Supplies *Cardstock, stickers and pen:* American Crafts; *Patterned paper:* Heidi Grace Designs; *Stamps and pearl accents:* Hero Arts; *Ink:* Memories, Stewart Superior Corporation; *Clip:* Stampin' Up!; *Adhesive, decorative scissors and punches:* Fiskars Americas; *Other:* Thread.

FINISH IT FASTER!
Stamp pretty trees and top them with pearl accents.

Looking for a fresh idea for your holiday pages? Look no **FURTHER**. Trim and adhere patterned paper to a cardstock background. Attach photos. Punch a scalloped border to add alongside the photos, then **CLIP** a clever block above it with journaling. Add a stamped title block with eye-catching white letter stickers.

The Birthday Girl | Suzy Plantamura

Supplies *Patterned paper:* Scenic Route; *Letter stickers:* Doodlebug Design, KI Memories and SEI; *Flowers:* Tinkering Ink; *Fiber:* Bazzill Basics Paper, Making Memories and unknown; *Rickrack:* Maya Road; *Pens:* EK Success and Newell Rubbermaid; *Adhesive:* Duncan Enterprises, EK Success and Glue Dots International; *Other:* Chipboard number. **Bright ideas:** Use colorful rickrack as a balloon "string." Wrap it around the number being celebrated. Help visually differentiate photos by adding white borders with a pen.

FINISH IT FASTER!
Substitute pieces of striped patterned paper for the fibers.

Save money by creating custom embellishments for your pages. Cut cardstock in the desired shape (a balloon and zigzag border here). Cover the cardstock with glue and attach fibers in a straight or **ZIGZAG** pattern. Trim off fiber ends. Showcase three photos (slightly offset), **MIX** letter stickers for an eye-catching title, and journal below the zigzag border.

4-wheelin'

Grandma got this electric car at a garage sale. She thought you and your sisters would have lots of fun playing with it. She was right. You and your sisters kept fighting over who would get the next turn. The next step is to get on a real four wheeler. Of the three of you, I'm sure that you would be adventurous enough to try it!

4-Wheelin' | Amy Alvis

Supplies *Cardstock:* Bazzill Basics Paper; *Patterned paper, vinyl stickers and felt flower:* American Crafts; *Font:* 2Peas Weathered Fence; *Adhesive:* 3L.

FINISH IT FASTER!
To shave off time, journal by hand.

Pump up the contrast with **SCALLOPED** paper and **ROUNDED** corners set against a dark background. Add photos, a title and journaling, then finish up with a die-cut design at right.

Here's a great way to display those 4" x 6" photos in a way young children can enjoy: Create a set of alphabet flashcards with your photos. Be sure to use photos with strong focal points so children can easily see what each letter is referencing.

how to make them:

> Select photos with strong focal points.
> Embellish with letter stamps, stickers or digital brushes.
> Laminate the photos.
> Tie them with a ribbon to keep the set of cards together.

try this too:

You can also make flashcards out of extra vacation photos, or go on a photo field trip and take shots of things that catch your child's interest.

—by britney mellen

flashcards

Baby Flashcards | britney mellen

Supplies *Software:* Adobe Photoshop CS3, Adobe Systems; *Digital brush:* Monogrammed Blocks Digital Stamps by Kellie Mize, *www.designerdigitals.com.*

GREAT DESIGN IN NO TIME

The timesaving payoff from using uncropped 4" x 6" photos is undeniable, but working with this size can present some special design challenges. How do you create beautiful pages *and* save time? Below, a few of our 2009 Dream Team members weigh in with some tips for achieving great looks with your "straight from the photo lab" prints.

MAGGIE HOLMES: Go for a two-page spread—you can get more pictures on your layout and still have lots of room for embellishments and great design.

EMILY FALCONBRIDGE: Sand the edges of your photos to create a slight "border" to help them stand out against your background and to create unity among the pictures on the layout.

CINDY TOBEY: Add a flip book to your layout to include more photos. (An envelope or accordion-style book works well, too.)

SUZY PLANTAMURA: Apply border stickers to a strip of photos to tie them all together and to give them a coordinated feel.

KELLY PURKEY: To save room on your page, add the title or journaling right on top of your photos in areas you would normally want to crop out.

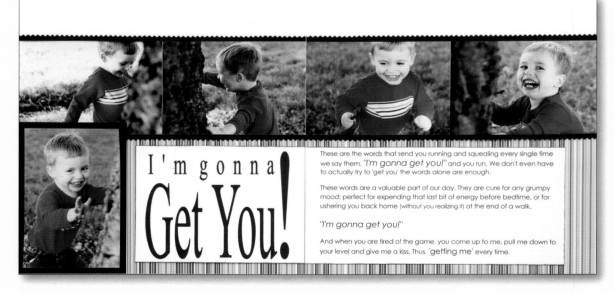

I'm Gonna Get You | April Peterson

Supplies *Cardstock:* Bazzill Basics Paper; *Patterned paper:* Chatterbox; *Ink:* ColorBox, Clearsnap; *Font:* Century Gothic and Times New Roman; *Other:* Adhesive and decorative-edged scissors.

Unhidden Beauty | Kendra McCracken

Supplies *Cardstock:* Bazzill Basics Paper; *Brads and jump rings:* Junkitz; *Acrylic letters:* Heidi Swapp for Advantus; *Canvas label:* 7gypsies; *Stamps:* PSX Design and Duncan Enterprises; *Ink:* Fluid Chalk, Clearsnap; StazOn, Tsukineko; *Ribbon:* C.M. Offray & Son; *Embroidery floss:* DMC; *Other:* Acrylic paint, adhesive, buttons, fabric, flowers and rhinestones.

At the Patch | Kelly Purkey

Supplies *Cardstock and pen:* American Crafts; *Patterned paper:* American Crafts (green stripe) and Heidi Grace Designs (orange); *Transparency:* Hambly Screen Prints; *Stamps and rhinestones:* Hero Arts; *Ink:* Stampin' Up!; *Chipboard:* Heidi Grace Designs; *Punches and adhesive:* Fiskars Americas.

becky higgins

from camera to composition

Here's a little expert advice from Becky on creating layouts with 4" x 6" photos. Follow her creative process in this Q & A to see how she puts a layout together.

Q What is the story behind these pictures?

A This group of photos is from our family's recent visit to historical Nauvoo, Illinois.

Q How did you choose the photos you used on this layout?

A I had already created a layout about specific sites in Nauvoo, so I wanted to use a few miscellaneous photos we took around the village. I picked the photos that best reminded me of our experience—those that represent the many wonderful people and rich history of Nauvoo.

Q How did you choose the colors and embellishments for your layout?

A I really wanted the pictures to speak for themselves, and I didn't feel that adding a lot of embellishments would help tell about our experience. This layout turned out exactly how I envisioned—clean and simple, with the focus on the photos.

Statues

Family pictures

Buildings

Signs

Roads and paths

Around Nauvoo | becky higgins

Supplies *Cardstock:* Bazzill Basics Paper; *Ink:* ColorBox, Clearsnap; *Brads:* American Crafts; *Font:* CK Newsprint, downloaded from *www. scrapnfonts.com.*

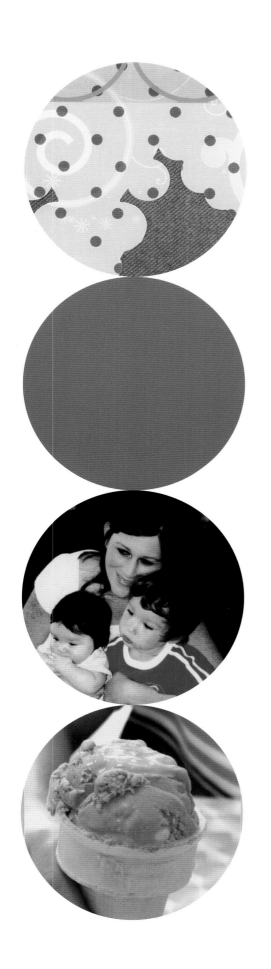

layouts with

4

photos

Our Santa Visit Gone Bad | Allison Davis

Supplies *Cardstock:* Bazzill Basics Paper; *Patterned paper:* BasicGrey; *Letter stickers:* Doodlebug Design and SEI; *Die cuts:* Cloud 9 Design, Fiskars Americas; *Stickers:* 7gypsies; *Chipboard star:* Imagination Project; *Ribbon:* C.M. Offray & Son and May Arts; *Ink:* ColorBox Fluid Chalk, Clearsnap; *Spray ink:* Tattered Angels; *Embroidery floss:* DMC; *Font:* Century Gothic; *Adhesive:* All Night Media, Therm O Web and Scrapbook Adhesives by 3L. **Bright idea:** Create a handmade tree with scraps of felt, and stitch a tree "garland" with embroidery floss.

FINISH IT FASTER!
Create an instant scallop by placing punched circles beneath a strip.

I really don't know what went wrong with our trip to see Santa. Drew was fine waiting in the line. Actually he was excited and talked about what he was going to say to Santa. When we rounded the corner and could finally see him, Drew got very quiet. When it was our turn, Drew refused to even look at him. I was standing with my camera up to my eye waiting for that perfect picture opportunity while Mike sat him down on Santa's lap. You would have thought that Mike had set Drew down in a pit of snakes by the sound of him. Santa was very patient and did his best to calm Drew but it just wasn't happening. I think the whole visit lasted about ten seconds. Later that evening when we walked by Santa as we were leaving the mall Drew said in a low grumbly voice, "Santa's stupid!" I think we'll just skip the Easter bunny this year.

GRINCH ALERT

Group photos, **EMBELLISHMENTS** and journaling strips on cardstock (a great timesaver!). Run a patterned-paper strip across the background to create a visual base. Top off the design with a holly-jolly **CHRISTMAS** tree made from 2" strips of layered ribbon or paper.

Eat Cake | Jennifer Armentrout

Supplies *Cardstock:* Bazzill Basics Paper; *Patterned paper:* BasicGrey, Collage Press, October Afternoon and Pink Paislee; *Chipboard:* Scenic Route; *Tag:* Creative Imaginations; *Brads and photo turns:* American Crafts; *Letter stickers:* October Afternoon; *Spray ink:* Maya Road; *Pen:* Sakura; *Adhesive:* 3M. **Bright idea:** Cut, stack and arrange chipboard pieces to create embellishments that fit your theme. Sand and ink the edges for definition.

Combine products in unique ways for one-of-a-kind accents. **MIST** cardstock with spray ink, then overlap and adhere two pieces of patterned paper (one torn). Attach photos, leaving the side of one unadhered to slide a journaling card underneath. Make a "cake piece" with a chipboard frame, **HEARTS** and a creative flame design.

FINISH IT FASTER!

Set a timer for 30 minutes—it will help you stay focused.

Johnny Rockets | Kelly Purkey

Supplies *Cardstock and patterned paper:* American Crafts; *Stickers:* Doodlebug Design; *Stamps:* Hero Arts; *Ink:* StazOn, Tsukineko; *Epoxy stickers:* Cloud 9 Design, Fiskars Americas; *Circle cutter, punches and adhesive:* Fiskars Americas; *Font:* SP Strut.

FINISH IT FASTER!
Give a journaling block "oomph" with a punched border.

Stamps and punches are great investments because you can use them over and over to create a multitude of looks. **MOUNT** photos on white cardstock, then adhere to a patterned-paper background. Add a journaling block and punched-circle accents decorated with a rubber stamp and **EPOXY** stickers.

Batting Practice | Ria M. Mojica

Supplies *Patterned paper:* October Afternoon; *Chipboard letters:* American Crafts; *Journaling sticker:* Collage Press; *Label maker:* Dymo; *Ink:* Clearsnap; *Pen:* Zig Writer, EK Success; *Adhesive:* 3M.

Numbering a **SERIES** of shots is a great way to show the order of events. Fan out photos on a background, showing them in sequence. Attach a wide **JOURNALING** strip and use it for a title as well as journaling, and add circle numbers.

FINISH IT FASTER!
Overlap nonessential areas on prints to save photo-editing time.

Ba Sketti, Be Happy | Missy Crowell

Supplies *Patterned paper:* foof-a-La, Autumn Leaves; *Letter stickers:* Doodlebug Design; *Stitch stamp:* Hero Arts; *Ink:* Marcella by Kay; *Adhesive:* Tombow; *Other:* Pen and thread. **Bright idea:** In need of a letter? Substitute a computer-generated letter in a different size.

Sketches are great tools for putting your scrapbooking on the fast track. Start with a simple **SKETCH**, altering as needed. (The second page here mirrors the first page.) Add photos and stitch them in place. Add paper strips, title letters and journaling. Fill some empty space with subtle **STITCH** designs—these resemble spaghetti.

FINISH IT FASTER!
Use a pen to create a stitch design on paper strips.

Clam Chowder for Lunch | Kelly Purkey

Supplies *Cardstock and pen:* American Crafts; *Patterned paper and stickers:* Heidi Grace Designs; *Stamps:* A Muse Art Stamps (public market) and Hero Arts (pattern and word bubble); *Ink:* Memories, Stewart Superior Corporation; *Epoxy stickers:* Cloud 9 Design, Fiskars Americas; *Circle cutter, punches and adhesive:* Fiskars Americas; *Other:* Thread. **Bright idea:** Stamp a word bubble for a novel way to add journaling.

FINISH IT FASTER!
Instead of stamping, use fun premade embellishments.

Position photos in a block (a **NO-FAIL** page design strategy!), then trim patterned paper to fill the remaining page background. Cut circles for the title and add letter stickers. Punch **DECORATIVE** stars, stamp a pattern onto cardstock and punch with a scallop border punch. Stamp, color and adhere additional designs.

Apples to Apples | Kelly Purkey

Supplies *Cardstock and brads:* American Crafts; *Patterned paper:* BasicGrey (vegetables) and Scenic Route (green and red); *Stickers:* Doodlebug Design; *Stamps and ink:* Stampin' Up!; *Epoxy stickers:* Cloud 9 Design, Fiskars; *Decorative scissors, punches and adhesive:* Fiskars Americas; *Font:* 2Peas Uncle Charles; *Other:* Thread.

FINISH IT FASTER!

Using stamped images in place of letters in a title is both cute and a great alternative to a traditional title.

Got a favorite family game? Why not devote a page to it? Trim and adhere patterned-paper **SECTIONS**, then attach three angled photos. Add cardstock strips and brads. Round corners of photo and mount on cardstock with similar rounding. Embellish with **STAMPS** and stickers.

Puri by Car | Mou Saha

Supplies *Cardstock:* Die Cuts With a View; *Stamps:* Martha Stewart Crafts; *Ink:* Tsukineko; *Tag:* 7gypsies; *Brad:* Making Memories; *Embroidery floss:* DMC; *Pen:* American Crafts; *Adhesive:* Scotch, 3M; *Other:* Bells, crocheted flowers and ribbon.

FINISH IT FASTER!
No time to embroider? Draw flower stems with a pen.

- **INFORMATION** -

Intricately carved temples steeped in history.
Colorful handicrafted items from native artisans.
Display of aromatic indigenous spices.
Stacks of appetizing snack packs for the hungry
tourists. The colors, tastes, smells and sights
of Puri fulfilled our senses and made the
long drive completely worth it.

Add a new **DIMENSION** to your layout with sound effects. Attach four photos and run ribbon strips above and below. Stitch around the photos and ribbon. Stamp a title, then journal on a **TAG** and attach it with a brad. Feeling musical? Sew on mini bells. Adhere crocheted flowers and embroider simple stems.

Blue Ice Cream | Beth Opel

Supplies *Cardstock:* Bazzill Basics Paper; *Patterned paper:* American Crafts (popsicle), Cosmo Cricket (dot and cloud) and Sonburn (stripe); *Letters:* Creative Imaginations (small blue), GCD Studios (large blue) and SEI (yellow); *Felt accents:* Chatterbox; *Adhesive badge and brads:* American Crafts; *Lion sticker:* Little Yellow Bicycle; *Acrylic accent:* KI Memories; *Corner-rounder punch:* EK Success; *Font:* Calibri; *Adhesive:* 3M, Helmar and Scrapbook Adhesives by 3L; *Other:* Photo turns.

FINISH IT FASTER!
Simplify your title by sticking to one alphabet set.

BLUE ice cream! Who knew? Use photos and patterned-paper blocks to fill spaces on the page. Remember to leave common margins between all elements for a cohesive design. Draw attention to your focal-point photo by placing your title and journaling near it, and finish with **BRIGHT**, fun embellishment clusters to lead the eye around the layout.

Summer Vacation | kristi baumgarten

Supplies *Patterned paper and epoxy circles:* Provo Craft; *Metal tags and rub-ons:* Making Memories; *Felt flowers:* American Crafts; *Fabric tags:* K&Company; *Circle stickers:* Jone Hallmark, Creative Imaginations.

"I almost always *scrap* with 4" x 6" or smaller photos. I find that scrapping with smaller photos allows for *more* white space, which fits my style."

—KELLY NOEL

My Crazy Kids | stephanie vetne

Supplies *Cardstock:* Bazzill Basics Paper; *Patterned paper, rub-ons and die cuts:* Luxe Designs; *Letter stickers:* American Crafts, Scenic Route, Polar Bear Press and SEI; *Adhesive:* Memory Tape Runner and Super Tape, Therm O Web; *Pen:* American Crafts.

Place *four* horizontal 4" x 6" photos in the center of a 12" x 12" page.

C-Carve | jennifer armentrout

Supplies *Cardstock:* Bazzill Basics Paper; *Patterned paper:* BasicGrey (orange) and My Mind's Eye (paisley); *Chipboard numbers and letter "C":* Heidi Swapp for Advantus; *Chipboard circle:* Colorbök; *Circle stamp:* Carolee's Creations; *Ink:* Rubber Stampede, Delta Creative; *Circle punch:* Marvy Uchida; *Pen:* American Crafts.

Create *variety* by taking pictures of the same subject from different points of view.

Singstar | jamie harper

Supplies *Cardstock:* Bazzill Basics Paper; *Patterned paper:* Scenic Route; *Embroidery floss:* Jo-Ann Stores; *Fonts:* Agency FB, downloaded from *www.freefonts.com*; Perpetua Titling MT, downloaded from the Internet.

Swan Boats | erin lincoln

Supplies *Patterned paper:* Anna Griffin; *Stamps, paint and ribbon:* Making Memories; *Stamps:* Autumn Leaves and Stampin' Up!; *Ink:* StazOn, Tsukineko; *Punches:* McGill and EK Success; *Font:* Times New Roman, Microsoft.

"If I know I'll be making a *layout* with several cropped photos, I create the basic design in Adobe Photoshop Elements first. Once I know the *sizes* I want, I can print out the photos exactly how I'll want them on the actual layout. It's great because I don't use *extra* ink for the segments of the photos that would simply be cropped anyway."

—BRITTANY BEATTIE

Over | amanda probst

Supplies *Cardstock:* Prism Papers; *Pattered paper and pen:* American Crafts.

Put a *spin* on a layout by placing all of the elements at a slant.

Pierced | Mou Saha

Supplies *Cardstock:* Die Cuts With a View; *Patterned paper:* Cosmo Cricket and Rusty Pickle; *Stamps:* Inkadinkado (tags) and Studio G (date); *Rhinestones:* Die Cuts With a View (heart, crown and diva) and Rusty Pickle (round); *Embroidery floss:* DMC; *Pens:* American Crafts and EK Success; *Adhesive:* 3M and Therm O Web. **Bright idea:** Lengthen a journaling tag by drawing pen lines in the same color as the stamping ink.

FINISH IT FASTER!

Embellishing is quick when you add instant bling with ready-made rhinestone accents.

Attach **PHOTOS** to cardstock, overlapping one and varying the heights for variety. Add a title, accents and stitching. **STAMP** tags on patterned paper and add journaling, then cut the tags out and attach them below the journaling.

Enhance the
motion
effect in your photos
by having your subject
run toward you as
you snap pictures.

Laugh | autumn baldwin

Supplies *Cardstock:* Bazzill Basics Paper; *Patterned paper:* American Crafts; *Fonts:* BalirMDITC TT Med, Bodoni Svty and Two ITC TTBook, downloaded from the Internet.

Ridin' Barefoot | jeri hoag

Supplies *Cardstock:* Bazzill Basics Paper; *Patterned paper:* Reminisce; *Chipboard stars:* Heidi Swapp for Advantus; *Paint:* Plaid Enterprises; *Letter stickers:* American Crafts and KI Memories; *Font:* 2Peas Quirky, downloaded from *www.twopeasinabucket.com.*

great seats &
great friends
make for a great

OPENING day

the first game of the season
(Titans vs. Jets) and my
first NFL game ever —
Stephanies, too! We had so
much fun laughing @ the
crazy NY Jets fan above us,
crossing our fingers that
the weatherman was wrong
about imminent rain, &
listening to Rene explain the
game of football to Stephanie.
One good thing for me: I
learned way more about fantasy
football than I ever thought
I would! And, even though we
lost, it was a close scoring
game & we thoroughly
enjoyed ourselves!   2006

Opening Day | april foster

Supplies *Cardstock:* Bazzill Basics Paper; *Patterned paper:* Scenic Route; *Chipboard letters:* Heidi Swapp for Advantus; *Stickers:* Heidi Swapp for Advantus, K&Company and 7gypsies; *Rub-ons:* American Crafts; *Pens:* Zig Writer, EK Success; Uni-ball Signo, Sanford.

For a *change* from the norm, crop four horizontal 4" x 6" photographs down to 2" x 6".

Take multiple photos of one *event* or activity to show the progression of events.

politely pouring tea.

excavating "sugar."

lapping like a dog.

blowing bubbles.

tea party. boy style.

It started out so sweet. The boys rediscovered this tea set (purchased after some hunting to find one that wasn't pink or purple mind you) and decided to have a tea party, though Asher stubbornly insisted it be called a water party as he'll drink nothing else. After some creative pouring to fill the tea pot, they settled down at the little table in the kitchen (handy for crafts and things like this). Noah poured them both some "tea" and they proceeded to scoop pretend sugar into their cups (the "sugar" was also water). Normal, right? As I grabbed the camera to capture this sweet moment, they reminded me that they are truly boys as the spoons became "grabber nabbers" and began excavating the sugar rather than simply scooping it. To top it off, though, they began challenging each other to see who could lap the water out of the cup like a dog fastest and then who could blow the most bubbles in their cup without using their hands. Boys. 07.09.2006

Tea Party | amanda probst
Supplies *Cardstock:* Bazzill Basics Paper; *Fonts:* Fine Hand and Blue Plate Special, downloaded from *www.scrapvillage.com;* Century Gothic, Microsoft.

I seem to be missing in our photos lately. As a step toward remedying that, I made sure to get a shot of me with each of my guys today at the park. Still, I think they're the stars of the photos. I'm probably biased.

my guys

My Guys | amanda probst
Supplies *Cardstock:* Bazzill Basics Paper; *Patterned paper:* Scenic Route; *Tag:* FontWerks; *Felt letters and pen:* American Crafts; *Ribbon:* May Arts.

Summer Beauty | greta hammond

Supplies *Cardstock:* Bazzill Basics Paper; *Patterned paper:* Scenic Route and Creative Imaginations; *Chipboard letters:* Heidi Swapp for Advantus; *Rub-ons:* Scenic Route and Daisy D's Paper Co.; *Letter stickers:* Making Memories; *Font:* Times New Roman, Microsoft.

This summer we were lucky enough to witness the entire metamorphosis of a caterpillar to a monarch butterfly, in our very own backyard. Over the period of a few weeks we watched the caterpillar eat it's way through several milkweed leaves, then attach itself onto the silk screen at the top of the bucket. It made itself into a "J" shape and was ready to begin building it's cocoon. And just like magic, one morning we woke to find a bright green cocoon and no caterpillar. After about 14 days, our beautiful butterfly emerged, leaving its chrysalis behind. We guided it onto a nearby flower, and watched it slowly gain strength. When it grew strong enough, it flew away. They say the monarch returns to where it began. And frankly, I find a little joy, knowing we might see it again. What an incredible experience to witness.

Embellish
your focal-point photo with
a digital or rub-on frame.

8 Years Old | annette pixley

Supplies *Cardstock:* Bazzill Basics Paper; *Patterned paper:* Die Cuts With a View; *Chipboard letters and stickers:* Making Memories; *Brads:* Queen & Co.; *Letter die cuts:* Cricut, Provo Craft; *Font:* Benguiat Bk BT, downloaded from the Internet.

To *create* a balanced photo collage, line your photos up along an invisible center line.

Nature Walk | greta hammond

Supplies *Cardstock:* Bazzill Basics Paper (brown) and WorldWin (blue); *Patterned paper, chipboard letters and photo corners:* Scenic Route; *Brads:* American Crafts; *Rub-ons:* Gin-X, Imagination Project; *Font:* Times New Roman, Microsoft.

Sweet Sixteen | theresa jasper

Supplies *Cardstock:* Bazzill Basics Paper; *Patterned paper:* Scenic Route and Making Memories; *Letter stickers:* Scrapworks; *Chipboard accents:* Making Memories and Heidi Swapp for Advantus; *Eyelets:* Making Memories; *Acetate shapes, gems, rub-ons and silhouette images:* Heidi Swapp for Advantus; *Stickers:* 7gypsies; *Pen:* Zig Memory System, EK Success; *Other:* Thread.

happy.

For Holden's third birthday, he picked out baseball plates & patriotic balloons, I made baseball cupcakes, and Rickey made homemade ice cream. We had a big cookout at Granny & PawPaw Moorefield's house with about 25 people. Holden received many presents, including an electric John Deere Gator and lots of sports toys. Holden was so excited! As he opened his gifts he said, "Oh, thank you, thank you everyone!" He fell asleep watching fireworks that evening.

party.cake.gifts.

Happy | lisa moorefield
Supplies *Cardstock:* Bazzill Basics Paper; *Velvet paper, letter stickers and epoxy frame:* SEI; *Font:* Franklin Gothic Medium, Microsoft.

"Last Christmas, my *mom* snapped a few dozen digital photographs of my family enjoying the holiday. I was happy and surprised when I arrived home and found a fun treat in my e-mail inbox—Mom had already *created* a wonderful Christmas album with the easy (and affordable) digital album templates at Smilebox (*www.smilebox.com*). It was so nice to print the pages she'd made and just slip them into an album."

—RACHEL THOMAE

Crop three photos into 4" x 4" *squares* and adhere them to your layout in three columns. Crop a fourth photo to embellish the title.

PHOTO-CORNER FINESSE

Add personality to your photos with these cute options.

Photo corners, those little attachments originally designed to anchor photos to the pages of scrapbooks and photo albums, now seem to be as much about style as they are about functionality. Whether you prefer the practicality of traditional corners, desire the chic appeal of faux corners or want to make your own unique corner creations, you'll discover a number of creative options.

Traditional Photo Corners

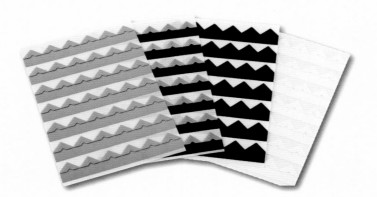

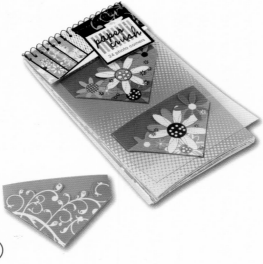

1

Adhesive

Scrapbook Adhesives by 3L
Scrapbook-Adhesives.com
Subtly hold any pic in place with these traditional corners, which are self-adhesive and come in several colors.

3

Paper

Martha Stewart Crafts
MarthaStewartCrafts.com
Pretty up any picture with these patterned beauties. Simply use a little adhesive to adhere them to your layout.

2

Die Cuts

Colorbök
Colorbok.com
Make a bold statement with any of the jumbo corners included in this sassy booklet.

Creative Corners

With just a bit of creativity and a few supplies from your stash, you can add even more photo options to your line-up.

FOLD RIBBON

Turn your leftover scraps of ribbon into the perfect photo frill.

(1) Cut two strips of ribbon to approximately 3".

(2) Add small amount of adhesive to center of each strip and fold ribbon in half to form corner.

(3) Trim ribbon ends at an angle. (Buttons are optional.)

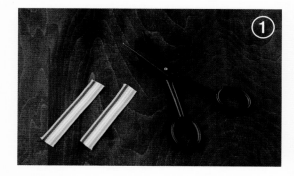

ATTACH BRADS

Build brad corners for a little texture and depth.

1. Select an assortment of brads (approximately five for each corner).

2. Pierce holes around corners of image.

3. Attach brads.

BEAD IT

Add a little sparkle to any image with bitty beads.

(1) Affix double-sided adhesive to corners of cardstock. (We used Super Tape by Therm O Web.)

(2) Cut cardstock at an angle to form corners.

(3) Pull up adhesive backing and dip corners in small dish of beads until thoroughly covered.

ali edwards

from
camera to
composition

Here's a little expert advice from Ali on creating layouts with 4" x 6" photos. Follow her creative process in this Q & A to see how she puts a layout together.

Q What is the story behind these pictures?

A These photos are from an adventure my son, Simon, took with his grandparents on the Oregon coast.

Q How did you choose the photos you used on this layout?

A One of the things I loved was that my mom took photos that were both up close and far away. The faraway photos, which show more environment, tell a completely different story than the close-up photos.

One of the main reasons I chose the tight photo of Simon's head is that there was room within that photo for my journaling. I like finding photos with white space that I can use as a home for my words.

Q How did you choose the colors and embellishments for your layout?

A My favorite accents and embellishments are words. Words and photos are the heart of it for me. I add a few other design elements here and there, but keeping the focus on the story and the words never leads me down the wrong path.

For the colors, I let the soft, muted colors of the Oregon coast inspire the shades of blue in my patterned-paper picks.

On the beach

Coastal scenes

Water fun

On the coast

Boats

Horizontal photos

Close-ups

Adventure | ali edwards, photos by pati mcdougall

Supplies *Cardstock:* Bazzill Basics Paper; *Patterned paper:* My Mind's Eye, Hambly Studios and Li'l Davis Designs; *Chipboard letters and pen:* American Crafts; *Graphic circular stamp:* 7gypsies; *Decorative paper border:* Doodlebug Design.

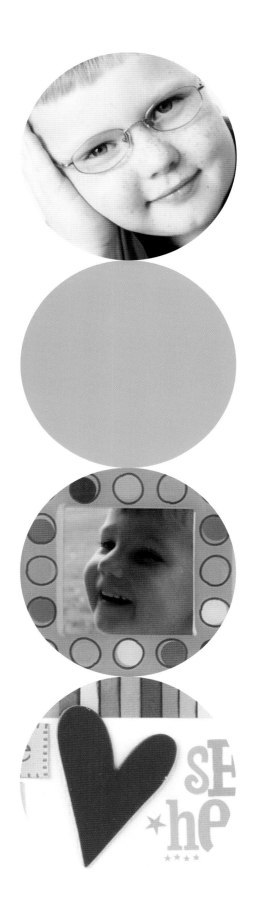

layouts
with

5

photos

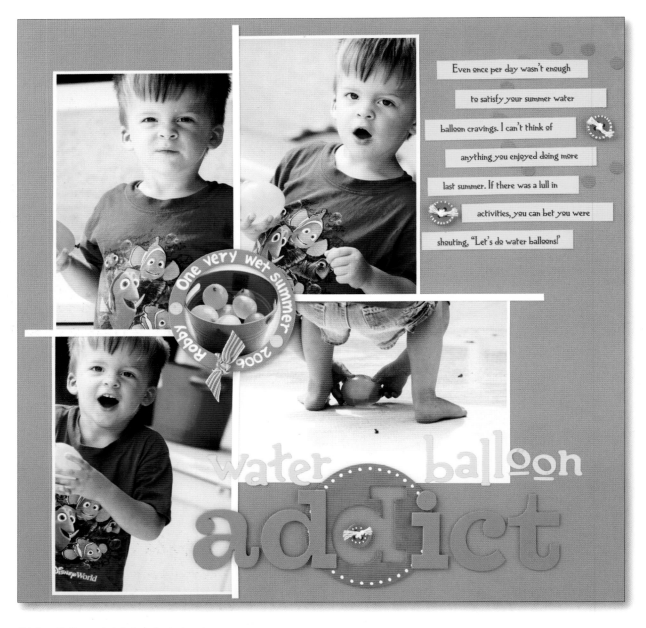

Even once per day wasn't enough to satisfy your summer water balloon cravings. I can't think of anything you enjoyed doing more last summer. If there was a lull in activities, you can bet you were shouting, "Let's do water balloons!"

One very wet summer
Robby 2006

water balloon addict

Water Balloon Addict | linda harrison

Supplies *Cardstock:* Bazzill Basics Paper; *Chipboard letters:* Creative Imaginations; *Chipboard circle:* Fancy Pants Designs; *Buttons:* Jo-Ann Stores; *Letter die cuts:* Zoe, QuicKutz; *Paint:* Pebbles Inc.; *Ribbon:* KI Memories; *Hole punch:* Fiskars; *Embroidery floss:* Making Memories; *Pen:* Sharpie, Sanford; *Font:* Gandy Dancer, downloaded from the Internet.

Perfect Fall Day | summer fullerton

Supplies *Cardstock:* Bazzill Basics Paper; *Patterned paper, chipboard flourishes and ribbon:* Fancy Pants Designs; *Stickers and rub-ons:* Arctic Frog; *Date tag and safety pin:* Making Memories; *Brads:* Queen & Co.; *Label tape:* Dymo; *Embroidery floss:* DMC; *Paint:* Plaid Enterprises; *Font:* SandraOH, downloaded from the Internet.

When creating a
series
of five photographs,
feature one close-up
of your subject.

"Frames are a great way to *highlight* your focal-point photo. Experiment with different types of materials for frames—try using ribbon, rick-rack, a string of beads, twine, strips of wire mesh or strips of fabric. You can even place small round or square *items* in a row around the photo (for example, eyelets, buttons, brads, grommets, beads or charms). For a quick, handmade touch, simply doodle with a pen around the edges of the photo!"

—LISA IVEY

Signs | courtney kelly
Supplies *Cardstock:* Bazzill Basics Paper; *Patterned paper and pen:* American Crafts; *Chipboard letters:* Scenic Route; *Font:* Century Gothic, Microsoft; *Other:* Corner-rounder punch.

Add *drama* to your 4" x 6" focal-point photo by cropping the rest of your photos. For extra emphasis, mat it on cardstock and doodle along the edges for a quick frame.

"Ever since a coworker told me about *Picasa* I've been addicted! This free photo-organizing software (*www.picasaweb.google.com*) allows you to quickly and easily manipulate your favorite *photos* with just a click of your mouse. You can choose from a variety of photo effects, such as soft focus, warmify or glow, to transform so-so photos in a matter of seconds!"

—VANESSA HOY

Pool Fun | pam callaghan

Supplies *Cardstock:* Bazzill Basics Paper; *Patterned paper:* American Crafts; *Flower die cut:* My Mind's Eye; *Rub-on letter and sticker:* Scenic Route; *Chipboard letters:* Pressed Petals; *Transparency:* Hammermill; *Font:* Abadi MT Condensed, Microsoft.

Idea to note: Pam chose a white background to help these action photos stand out.

Show *action* in a series of five photos. Try cropping each one to create a unique shape on your layout.

It's Just Me | hillary heidelberg

Supplies *Cardstock:* Bazzill Basics Paper; *Patterned paper, word sticker and ribbon:* Making Memories; *Chipboard letters:* Heidi Swapp for Advantus; *Rub-on letters:* American Crafts; *Font:* MKAbel, downloaded from *www.dafont.com*.

Wayfarers Chapel | susan opel

Supplies *Cardstock:* Bazzill Basics Paper; *Patterned paper, rub-on letters and words:* Scenic Route; *Paper flowers:* Prima; *Brads:* Making Memories and Creative Impressions; *Pen:* Zig Millennium, EK Success; *Fonts:* AL Uncle Charles, downloaded from *www.twopeasinabucket.com*; PR8 Charade, downloaded from the Internet.

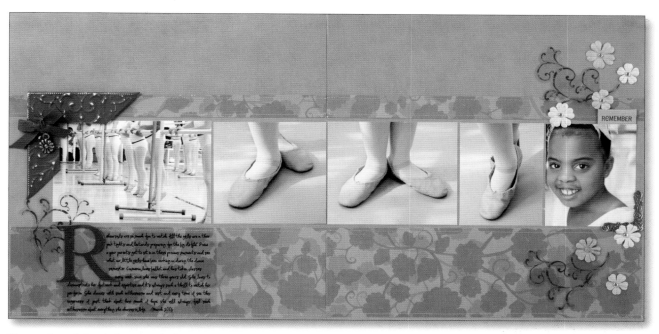

Remember | lisa tutman-oglesby

Supplies *Patterned paper:* Chatterbox; *Flowers:* Prima; *Brads, metal frame, paint and small safety pin:* Making Memories; *Chipboard letter:* Heidi Swapp for Advantus; *Scroll transparency:* My Mind's Eye; *Woven label:* Scrapworks; *Tiny metal frame:* Nunn Design; *Font:* Susie's Hand, downloaded from the Internet; *Other:* Ribbon, thread, charm and transparency.

Arrange the *photos* on your page so they lead the viewer's eye to the focal-point photo. Then, embellish it with *accents* such as rub-on flourishes and flowers.

Bree | Joannie McBride

Supplies *Cardstock:* Bazzill Basics Paper; *Patterned paper, flower die cuts, journaling spot and tab:* My Mind's Eye; *Letter stickers:* American Crafts; *Ribbon and buttons:* Making Memories; *Circle punch:* Marvy Uchida; *Rub-on:* SEI; *Pens:* American Crafts and Sakura; *Adhesive:* Fiskars Americas; *Other:* Staples. **Bright idea:** Pinching pennies? Punch out circle accents from patterned paper.

FINISH IT FASTER!
Adorn with ready-made circle accents.

Bree -
I love how
easy-going and
fun loving you are.
you're one of the most
genuine and sincere
teen-agers I know.
Thank you for adding
"Sunshine" to my life.
I love you!
- the other mom !!
2009

Use photos from a variety of events that reveal your subject's **PERSONALITY**. Place the patterned paper on cardstock and adhere. Mat photos. Add ribbon, photos, punch-outs, a journaling spot and buttons. **STAPLE** the ribbon and tab and add title and rub-on.

Tea Party | Linda Rodriguez

Supplies *Software:* Adobe Photoshop, Lightroom; *Cardstock:* Bazzill Basics Paper; *Patterned paper and tags:* BasicGrey; *Ribbon:* American Crafts and Making Memories; *Velvet brad:* Making Memories; *Title letters and flourish:* Cricut Expression, Provo Craft; *Photo filter:* Creative Aged Photo Preset, Adobe; *Pen:* Sakura; *Adhesive:* EK Success and Glue Dots International; *Other:* Thread. **Bright idea:** Layer journaling shapes and write continuously across them.

FINISH IT FASTER!
Use stickers or chipboard for the title letters and flourish.

Use a photo filter to give pictures a soft, **TIMELESS** quality, then print the photos and affix them to cardstock. Fill in the empty spaces with patterned paper and adhere the block to the background paper. Add narrow, stitched paper strips above and below, highlighting them with strips of ribbon. Add a title, **FLOURISH** and journaling.

I've Been Looking at the Railroad | Andrea Friebus

Supplies *Cardstock:* Bazzill Basics Paper; *Patterned paper:* Chatterbox and My Mind's Eye; *Rub-ons:* Daisy D's Paper Co. and Kaisercraft; *Chipboard brackets:* Heidi Swapp for Advantus; *Flowers, chipboard circle and brads:* Making Memories; *Snaps:* We R Memory Keepers; *Staples and letter stamps:* EK Success; *Letter stickers:* American Crafts and Provo Craft; *Adhesive:* Therm O Web; *Other:* Ink, date stamp and photo turn.
Bright idea: To create a grungy, distressed look, be messy on purpose while stamping a title.

FINISH IT FASTER!
Cut a frame in half to make brackets, or diagonally to make photo corners.

Layer pieces of patterned paper, then adhere photos and add **DECORATIVE** elements, such as **BRACKETS**, rub-ons, snaps and staples.

The First Summer | Allison Davis

Supplies *Cardstock:* Bazzill Basics Paper; *Patterned paper:* Cosmo Cricket; *Letters:* American Crafts; *Chipboard flowers and pin:* Fancy Pants Designs; *Ribbon:* C.M. Offray & Son, Fancy Pants Designs and May Arts; *Circle punch:* EK Success; *Paint:* Making Memories; *Ink:* ColorBox Fluid Chalk, Clearsnap; *Pen:* Zig Writer, EK Success; *Adhesive:* Scrapbook Adhesives by 3L and Therm O Web.

FINISH IT FASTER!
Paint a title word a new color for emphasis.

Ink both photo and paper edges, then layer patterned papers on cardstock and embellish with ribbon, **CHIPBOARD** flowers and a stick pin. Heighten the sense of **WHIMSY** by adding chipboard flowers to patterned-paper circles (created with a punch). Add journaling and a title.

Sophie's favorite place to go is Laguna Beach. We walk around, go to the park to swing, eat at Johnny Rockets and take lots of photos! 08.08

a day in la

A Day in Laguna | Suzy Plantamura

Supplies *Cardstock:* Bazzill Basics Paper; *Patterned paper:* Creative Imaginations; *Chipboard letters:* Heidi Swapp for Advantus (orange), KI Memories (green and blue) and Scenic Route (white); *Flowers and stickers:* Creative Imaginations; *Journaling sheets and shapes:* Making Memories and My Mind's Eye; *Chipboard embellishments:* Heidi Grace Designs and KI Memories; *Brad:* Making Memories; *Adhesive:* Duncan Enterprises, EK Success and Glue Dots International. **Bright idea:** Cut a journaling tag in two and put one piece above your photo and one below.

FINISH IT FASTER!
Cut shapes from patterned paper to make circles, arrows and tags.

Cut patterned-paper pieces from scraps and layer them along the bottom of two pieces of cardstock. Leave room at left for journaling, then line up five **VERTICAL** photos at the top of the border. Mix various letters to create a title. Draw **CURVED** lines with a pen, then journal in between them.

Hanging Out with Dad | Suzy Plantamura

Supplies *Cardstock:* Die Cuts With a View; *Patterned paper:* October Afternoon (green and striped), Pink Paislee (reds and cream) and Sassafras (specialty border); *Chipboard cloud and square:* Pink Paislee; *Stickers:* October Afternoon; *Letters:* Doodlebug Design (brown) and Making Memories (ledger); *Flower stickers:* Heidi Grace Designs; *Felt flowers and button brads:* Making Memories; *Corner-rounder punch:* Creative Memories; *Ink:* ColorBox, Clearsnap; *Adhesive:* Duncan Enterprises, EK Success and Glue Dots International; *Other:* Cream brad. Bright idea: To create this journaling block, place sticker on top of chipboard accent and then cut the outside edge of the sticker to use behind as a border.

FINISH IT FASTER!
Leave the extra background in your photos and liven them with accents.

Beautiful fall days

I just adore these photos of Liz and Dad in Memorial Park. They were so silly when I was taking their pictures. It was a beautiful Fall day and we were all visiting Salt Lake for Dad's birthday. Dad was pushing the girls in the stroller while Liz pushed Billie. Hanging with dad→perfect.

it doesn't get any better than this

Remember   Salt Lake City October '02

After inking the edges and rounding two corners (which really helps to **DEFINE** the edges of your design), line up three pieces of 8" x 8" paper on top of cardstock. Add patterned paper below and in another layer. Adhere. Add photos and embellishments. (Choose which photo lends itself best to being divided between two pages.) Draw a page border on the cardstock and outline the title block for **OOMPH**.

Funny Flapjacks | Brigid Gonzalez

Supplies *Software:* Adobe Photoshop CS3; *Digital painted background:* Painterly Backgrounds No. 1 by Ali Edwards; *Fonts:* Benny Blanco (title), CK Becky (date) and Vegur (journaling). **Bright ideas:** Create the same look traditionally on white cardstock. Just paint a large background swatch and use rub-on letters for the white title. Also, sidestep the need to crop by getting in super close to your subject—then taking two steps forward—before taking the picture.

FINISH IT FASTER!
Cut out trimming time—print the completed journaling card on 4" x 6" photo paper with your photos.

INTERSPERSE detail shots with photos of people to tell the whole story. Stagger five photos evenly across the layout, tilting each slightly. Leave space for a 4″ x 6″ journaling tag. Type journaling on a 4″ x 6″ white rectangle, then add visual weight by drawing a red **BORDER** around the journaling. Add a title and journaling, then add a red border around the entire layout.

50 | Susan Opel | Photos by Carolyn McAfee

Supplies *Cardstock:* Bazzill Basics Paper (black) and WorldWin (tan); *Patterned paper:* The Paper Company; *Transparency:* Hambly Screen Prints; *Chipboard numbers:* Creative Imaginations; *Tag punches:* Marvy Uchida; *Gold metal dots:* Michaels; *Flower:* Daisy D's Paper Co.; *Gold metallic pen:* Newell Rubbermaid; *Font:* Century Gothic; *Adhesive:* Glue Dots International and Scrapbook Adhesives by 3L; *Other:* Adhesive pearl, black lace trim and gold accent. Bright idea: Use a ribbon border to lead the eye to your spotlight photograph.

FINISH IT FASTER!

Mimic the gold metallic dots with a gold pen.

With a little ingenuity, you can alter embellishments for a custom look. Arrange photos on cardstock. Paint chipboard numbers with a gold **METALLIC** pen and attach to a transparency with foam tape. Adhere the transparency (hiding the adhesive behind numbers) and patterned paper to cardstock. Add **LACE** trim and gold metallic dots. Print journaling on cardstock, then punch and mat on black cardstock. Embellish layout as desired.

photo clipboard frame

I like variety in my photo displays, so I love the idea of a frame that allows me to easily swap out different photos. I used a 7gypsies clipboard frame to create a fun family frame. Here's how:

1. Affix a chipboard bookplate phrase to the frame. I chose a generic phrase so I can swap out different family photos as desired.

2. Mat the photo on cardstock, then add a rub-on border.

3. Slip the photo into the frame and add a chipboard accent over the frame.

Variation: Create a great gift for a father or husband with a "Man of All Seasons" framed project, then switch out the photos with the seasons.

—by vanessa hoy

Family Clipboard | vanessa hoy

Supplies *Clipboard frame:* 7gypsies; *Paint:* Delta Creative; *Ribbon:* We R Memory Keepers; *"Family" bookplate accent:* me & my BIG ideas.

photo flip album

I love making the most of my supplies . . . so when I saw this spiral-bound album that doubles as a display, I knew it was perfect for showing off my favorite photos. Making it was a snap. Here's how:

1. Embellish the cover with a photo, patterned papers, ribbon and flowers, as desired.

2. Add the decorated pages to the album.

3. Display your favorite photo of the day by simply flipping to that page.

Variation: Decorate each page of your album by color. Then flip to the appropriate color that matches your mood, outfit or decor on any given day!

—by vanessa hoy

Emily Louise 2006 | vanessa hoy, photo by lesa paulson

Supplies *Album, patterned paper, flower and brad:* Making Memories; *Adhesive ribbon:* Die Cuts With a View; *Decorative pins:* Heidi Grace Designs.

Looking for a fun decor piece to display photos for that young 20-something in your family? This is the perfect addition to a craft room or bedroom. This vintage, whimsical photo display offers endless possibilities!

how to make this:

> Pin vintage photos to a dress form.
  Tip: If you're worried about damaging vintage photos, use duplicates instead.

> Embellish the dress form with flowers or pearls to match the room where it will be displayed.

try this too:

Use clothespins to attach photos to a wire dress form.

dress form

Vintage Memories Dress Form | britney mellen

Supplies *Dress form and pins:* Pottery Barn Teen; *Photos:* Downloaded from *www.designerdigitals.com; Other:* Pearls and fabric brooch.

jessica sprague

from camera to composition

Here's a little expert advice from Jessica on creating layouts with 4" x 6" photos. Follow her creative process in this Q & A to see how she puts a layout together.

Q What is the story behind these pictures?

A Our family took a Saturday afternoon walk in the woods near our new house last fall, and these photos were the result of that outing.

Q How did you choose the photos you used on this layout?

A I noticed a trend in the pictures: there were many where various members of the family were holding hands on the walk. My favorite part of the event—the part I wanted to capture—was the way we went hand in hand. I chose photos to support that theme.

Q How did you choose the colors and embellishments for your layout?

A I chose two green shades of cardstock as the main colors—they blended with the color in the leaves, and they didn't compete with the bright colors in my photos. I didn't want to lose the context of the beautiful forest, so I left all of my photos uncropped but added small embellishments to emphasize the subjects in the photos.

With Dad

On the trail

Heading home

With Mom

Playing in the leaves

Hand in Hand | jessica sprague

Supplies *Cardstock:* Bazzill Basics Paper; *Patterned paper and chipboard tags:* Scenic Route; *Chipboard brackets:* American Crafts; *Leaf and corner-rounder punches:* EK Success; *Fonts:* Steel Fish Outline (printed on patterned paper and hand-cut), downloaded from *www.myfonts.com*; Century Gothic, Microsoft.

Work with *different* angles to capture a particular pose. For example, while holding a child's hand, take a photo looking down from your perspective.

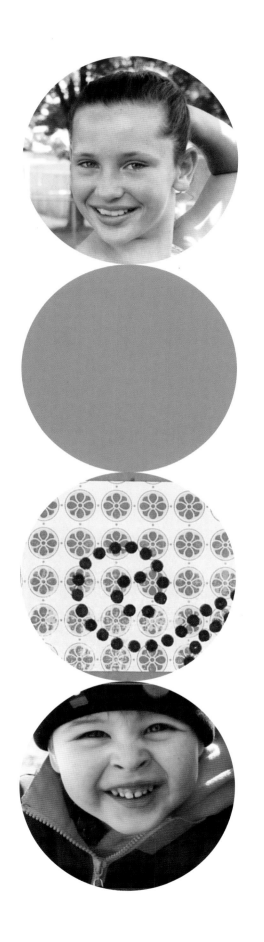

layouts
with

6 TO 7

photos

Since my parents are known for their master skills in the kitchen, I think we were all happy to drive to Aunt Judys for Thanksgiving dinner. Angela and Kevin were in town, and Kevin had told me the month before that he was looking forward to cooking the turkey. I don't usually like turkey but his was really juicy and good. There was also delicious ham, mashed potatoes, casseroles, and desserts. Lots of desserts! Pies and cake and little cupcakes. Amy made me a whole big container full of her famous cookies (one of my absolute favorite things to eat!!!) to take back to Chicago with me. It was a fun time sitting around and joking with family and eating such good food. A very happy Thanksgiving! Nov. 2008

Happy Thanksgiving | Kelly Purkey

Supplies *Cardstock:* American Crafts (pink) and Bazzill Basics Paper (kraft); *Patterned paper:* American Crafts (orange) and Doodlebug Design (teal); *Stickers:* American Crafts; *Stamps:* Hero Arts; *Ink:* Memories, Stewart Superior Corporation; *Punches and adhesive:* Fiskars Americas; *Font:* 2Peas Typo; *Other:* Thread.

FINISH IT FASTER!

No need for hunting for embellishments—add heart with stamped . . . hearts!

Trim and adhere orange patterned paper to a **KRAFT** cardstock background (kraft is a great all-purpose neutral). Machine-stitch around the outside. Line up several photos in a row and adhere. Add teal patterned paper, **CARDSTOCK** strips and journaling. Create a title.

Halloween 2007 | Katie Anaya

Supplies *Cardstock:* Bazzill Basics Paper; *Patterned paper:* BasicGrey; *Specialty paper:* KI Memories (die-cut); *Buttons:* Fancy Pants Designs; *Stamp:* 7gypsies; *Letter stickers:* American Crafts; *Adhesive:* 3-D Pop Dots, EK Success; Adhesive Photo Corners, Scrapbook Adhesives by 3L; *Other:* Chipboard, ribbon, felt border, pen and staples. **Bright idea:** Present one photo in black and white with a white border to set it off from the rest of your design.

FINISH IT FASTER!
Snip and staple ribbon lengths for a creative photo edge.

Celebrate pumpkins, fall fun and Halloween with a **FESTIVE** line-up of photos on cardstock. Add patterned paper and **LACE** cardstock to the center of the spread. Adhere photos, title felt and fall-colored buttons. Finish it up with a cute journaling spot and ribbon.

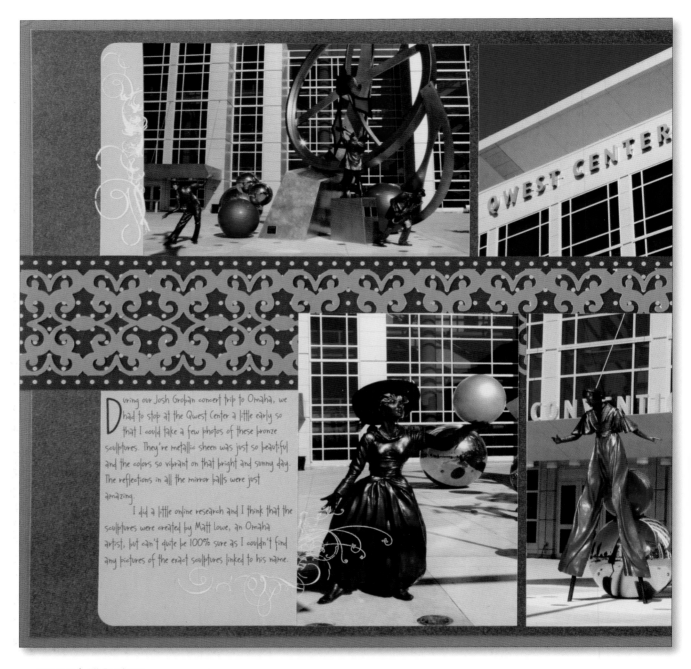

Bronze | Jill Paulson

Supplies *Cardstock:* Bazzill Basics Paper; *Patterned paper:* American Crafts; *Specialty paper:* Paper Wishes (shimmer) and KI Memories (die-cut); *Letter stickers:* Making Memories; *Rub-ons:* BasicGrey; *Corner-rounder punch:* Marvy Uchida; *Font:* Journaling Hand; *Adhesive:* Glue Dots International and Henkel Corporation. **Bright idea:** Let building signage serve as part of your title.

FINISH IT FASTER!
Trim die-cut paper to create paper lace.

Use specialty papers for a designer look in minutes. Begin with an **ORANGE** cardstock base, then add a blue **SHIMMER** paper with a finish similar to that of the statues pictured. Cut patterned paper and lace paper strips to connect the two-page layout, then adhere. Add a journaling block, photos and prominent letter stickers to complete the title.

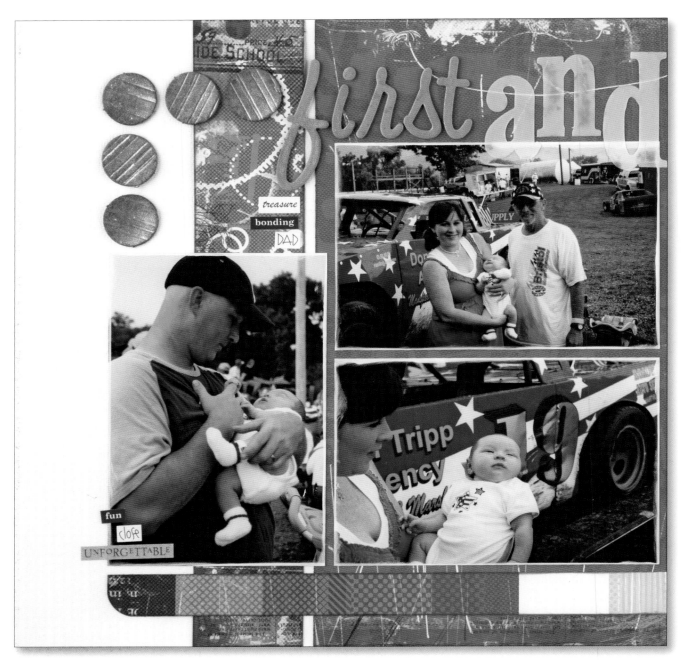

First and Last | Allison Davis

Supplies *Cardstock:* Bazzill Basics Paper; *Patterned paper:* Cosmo Cricket; *Letters:* BasicGrey (chipboard) and Maya Road (clear); *Flexible chipboard:* Grungeboard, Tim Holtz; *Word stickers:* 7gypsies, EK Success, K&Company and Making Memories; *Corner-rounder punch:* Fiskars Americas; *Paint:* Making Memories; *Ink:* ColorBox Fluid Chalk, Clearsnap; *Glimmer spray:* Tattered Angels; *Font:* American Typewriter; *Adhesive:* Glue Dots International and Scrapbook Adhesives by 3L. **Bright idea:** Create mirror-image pages by repeating the same photo arrangement, only flipped.

FINISH IT FASTER!
Ink photo edges white for instant distinction.

I would have never guessed that Drew's first trip to the race track would also be my dad's last. I had imagined years and years of Drew getting to watch his grandpa race and spending every weekend at the track. Every weekend covered in dirt. Every weekend getting the same plastic checkered flag to wave around. Every weekend eating stale nachos and drinking cold sodas. Every weekend learning more about racing. Every weekend sitting in those same wooden bleachers. Every weekend getting to experience what it was like to watch him race. Every weekend building a stronger bond with his grandpa. I am heartbroken knowing that Drew will never experience what all of that would be like.

Add vertical patterned-paper strips to **CARDSTOCK**, then position photos on top and adhere. Cut two horizontal strips, round one side on each, and ink the edges. Create a visual "rectangle" with the title, circles, **PHOTOS** and striped strip along the bottom.

Ka Pow | Ashley Horton

Supplies *Cardstock:* DMD, Inc.; *Eyelets:* Spare Parts; *Die-cut machine:* Cricut, Provo Craft; *Hole punch:* Crop-A-Dile, We R Memory Keepers; *Font:* Anime Ace; *Adhesive:* Plaid Enterprises and Scrapbook Adhesives by 3L; *Other:* Pen, comic strip clip art and ribbon. Bright idea: To create this journaling look in Microsoft Word, insert a text box and type all uppercase in a comic book–style font.

FINISH IT FASTER!
Use star stickers or star punches for a quick impact.

Plan a "comic book–look" layout, superhero style! Draw boxes in pen for some of the photos and clip art. To create the title block, machine-cut letters and overlap them on black cardstock. **ELEVATE** three letters with foam dots. Cut around the title block, then outline the yellow letters and burst with a thin black pen. Machine-cut the **STARS** and add white paper behind. Use the leftover blue stars elsewhere as accents.

Air and Space | Jill Paulson

Supplies *Cardstock:* Paperbilities; *Patterned paper:* BasicGrey and Mustard Moon; *Letter stickers:* BasicGrey; *Corner-rounder punch:* Marvy Uchida; *Ink:* ColorBox, Clearsnap; *Font:* Journaling Hand; *Adhesive:* Duck.

FINISH IT FASTER!
Use two sizes of circle punches to punch smaller circles out of larger circles.

No wide-format printer? No problem. Cut a piece of cardstock to accommodate **COMPUTER** journaling from a standard-sized printer. Round all four edges of the cardstock background and add photos. Position a patterned-paper strip **HORIZONTALLY** to hide cut marks (you can also use ribbon, fabric or a border sticker). Add title and circle embellishments.

My Girls | Joannie McBride

Supplies *Cardstock:* Bazzill Basics Paper; *Patterned paper, transparency, scalloped oval, circle die cut and journaling spot:* My Mind's Eye; *Paper flowers and brads:* Making Memories; *Letter stickers:* SEI; *Rub-ons and rhinestone brads:* American Crafts; *Pen:* Newell Rubbermaid; *Adhesive:* Fiskars Americas.

FINISH IT FASTER!
Switch out patterned papers to reflect a boy page or a baby page.

Brittany 19
Brianne 17
Ashley 17
Kaylee 10
2009

Here's an easy design for horizontal photos: Cut strips of **SCALLOP** cardstock and adhere them inside the outer edges of the patterned paper. Place three photos vertically in a row on each page. Add patterned-paper strips, **EMBELLISHMENTS** and journaling.

Remember | Joannie McBride

Supplies *Cardstock:* The Paper Company; *Patterned paper:* American Crafts (green) and Creative Imaginations (brown); *Rub-on letters and "explore" die cut:* We R Memory Keepers; *Journaling tag and rhinestone brads:* Making Memories; *Flowers:* The Paper Studio; *Rhinestones:* KitoftheMonth.com; *Pen:* Newell Rubbermaid; *Adhesive:* Fiskars Americas. **Bright idea:** Go over letters with a pen to help a rub-on title stand out more.

FINISH IT FASTER!
Trim same-size photo mats in advance for quick assembly.

Use sections of patterned paper to ground your design. **ADHERE** two 3" x 12" patterned-paper strips to a cardstock background. Overlap each strip with an 11" x 1" patterned-paper strip. Mat photos with cardstock, then adhere them to the layout. Add a rub-on title and phrase, **FLOWERS**, tag, rhinestones and journaling.

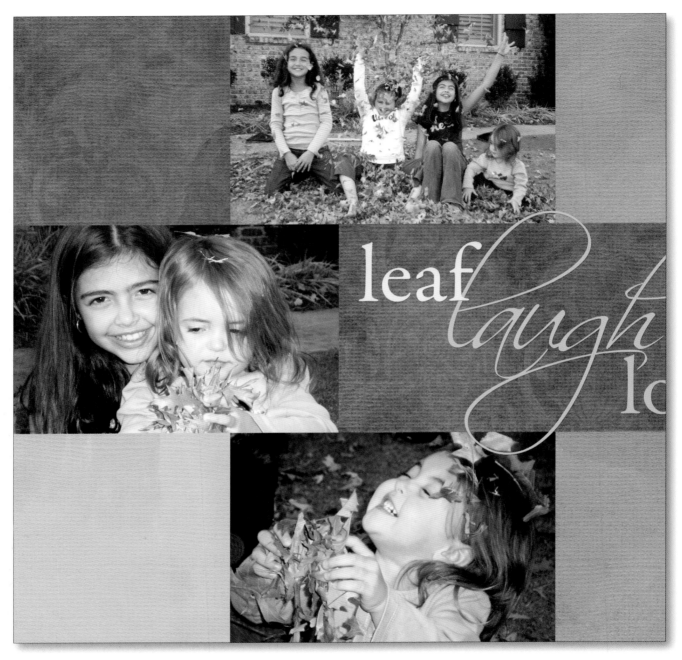

Leaf, Laugh, Love | Brigid Gonzalez

Supplies *Software:* Adobe Photoshop CS3; *Digital papers:* Harvest Moon kit by Amanda Dykan and Melissa Bennett; *Fonts:* Adobe Garamond and Scriptina.

FINISH IT FASTER!
Use rub-ons to get the look of a script font overlaying the photos.

Playing in the leaves is always one of the best things about the fall. Though we don't have a super-huge yard, we always end up with plenty of leaves to rake into piles just before you girls jump in and toss them around again. It's always nice to see you outside and having fun, unplugged from all of your gadgets and gizmos, breathing in the fresh air.

Create a new 24″ x 12″ document (300 dpi) in Adobe Photoshop. Add your **PHOTOS** as desired to your digital document. Place **DIGITAL** patterned papers and add a title and journaling. Not a digital scrapper? Use this design for a traditional layout.

{2400} | sandi minchuk

Supplies *Cardstock:* Bazzill Basics Paper; *Patterned paper and rub-on letters:* Chatterbox; *Page tabs:* KI Memories; *Letter stickers:* Doodlebug Design and KI Memories; *Fonts:* Times New Roman, Microsoft; P22 Garamouche, downloaded from *www.p22.com.*

"When photographing a *birthday* party, I remind myself to take a good assortment of close-up shots (the gifts, the birthday cake, the birthday child) and wide-angle shots (party decorations, party guests, party games). It's easier to create a layout that tells a story when you have a *good* variety of shots to scrapbook."

—RACHEL THOMAE

On the Bump | linda rodriguez

Supplies *Software:* PhotoDraw 2.0, Microsoft; *Digital patterned paper:* Project 26—Xmas Island by Tracy Ann Robinson, *www.scrapbook-bytes.com*; Schnookums by Laura Deacetis, *www.sweetshoppedesigns.com*; *Digital ribbon, ring, twine, screws, staples and alphabet:* Schnookums by Laura Deacetis, *www.sweet-shoppedesigns.com*; *Digital cardboard star:* Hard @ Play Kit by Dani Mogstad, *www.sweetshoppedesigns.com*; *Digital paint stroke:* Stacy McFadden; *Digital date stamp:* Amber Clegg, *www.scrapartist.com*; *Font:* Times and Times Again, downloaded from *www.dafont.com*.

The Hunt | kelly noel

Supplies *Cardstock:* Bazzill Basics Paper; *Patterned paper, chipboard brackets and foam letters:* American Crafts; *Ribbon:* Fancy Pants Designs; *Font:* Primary, downloaded from *www.momscornerforkids.com*.

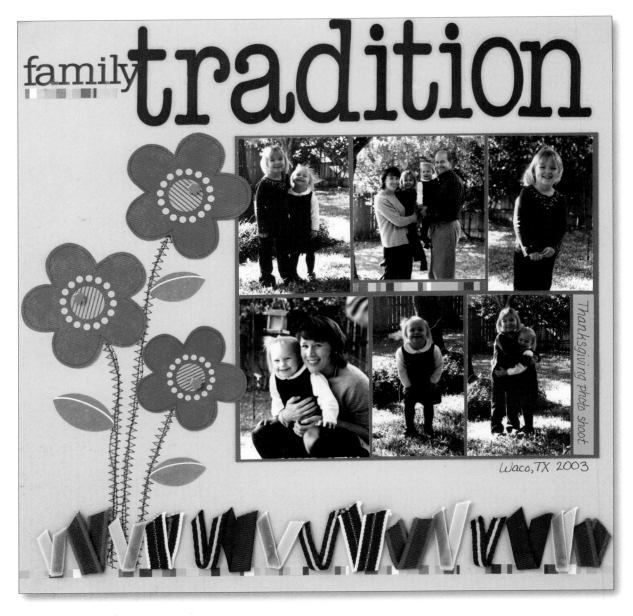

Family Tradition | lisa dorsey

Supplies *Cardstock:* Bazzill Basics Paper; *Patterned paper:* Mustard Moon; *Brads and ribbon:* Self-Addressed; *Letter stickers:* American Crafts (small) and Mustard Moon (large); *Pen:* Zig Millennium, EK Success.

Keep photos from getting lost on a layout by cropping them into a block.

H2O Happy | annette pixley

Supplies *Patterned paper and letters:* Crate Paper; *Chipboard flower and circular accent :* Gin-X, Imagination Project; *Photo turns and brads:* Queen & Co.; *Sequins, flowers and paper frills:* Doodlebug Design; *Letter stickers:* EK Success; *Rub-ons:* KI Memories; *Font:* 2Peas Goofball, downloaded from *www.twopeasinabucket.com*.

"I find that 4" x 6" photos are the *perfect* size for most every layout—they're large enough to capture the full detail of the photos but not too large that they overwhelm the page."

—ANNETTE PIXLEY

Go Blue | beth opel

Supplies *Cardstock:* Bazzill Basics Paper (white) and Prism Papers (blue); *Patterned paper:* Boxer Scrapbook Productions; *Daisy embellishment:* Jesse James & Co.; *Brads:* Making Memories; *Felt:* Jo-Ann Stores; *Fonts:* Arial Narrow (journaling) and Rage Italic (title), Microsoft.

"When I *design* with 4" x 6" prints, I love to place them in vertical or horizontal strips on my layout. The strips help me fit more photos on the page and *maintain* a nice balance."

—BRITTANY BEATTIE

D Is for Difficult | erin lincoln

Supplies *Patterned paper:* My Mind's Eye and Scrapworks; *Stickers:* Chatterbox and KI Memories; *Metal tag and brad:* Making Memories; *Stamps:* FontWerks and Limited Edition Rubber Stamps; *Rub-ons:* Heidi Grace for Fiskars; *Pen:* Sharpie, Sanford; *Other:* Photo corners and binder clips.

"Don't forget to take lots of *candid* and unstaged photos—not all pictures have to be posed. It's a great way to capture the true *spirit* or feeling of the moment."

—RACHEL THOMAE

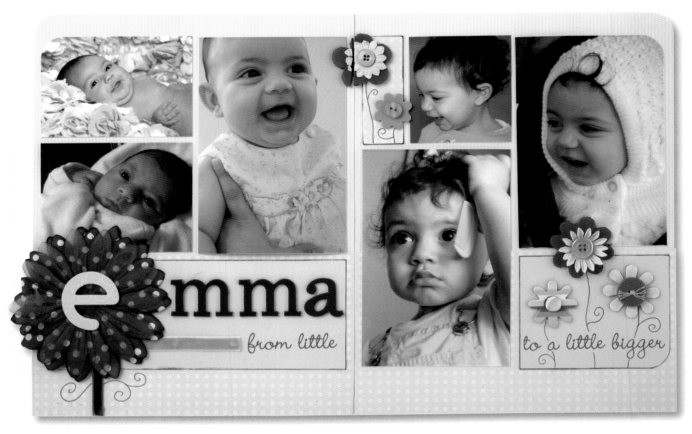

Emma | beth opel

Supplies *Cardstock:* Bazzill Basics Paper; *Patterned paper, chipboard "e" and flowers:* KI Memories; *Leather flowers, velvet ribbon and paper flower:* Making Memories; *Brown chipboard letters:* Heidi Swapp for Advantus; *Button with thread and corner-rounder punch:* EK Success; *Silk flowers:* Petaloo (large brown dot); *Ink:* Tim Holtz Distress Ink, Ranger Industries; *Pen:* Zig Millennium, EK Success; *Font:* Wendy Medium, downloaded from *www.dafont.com*; *Other:* Buttons and small silk flowers.

"Almost all of my pages *begin* with 4" x 6" photos. I find it's easier to just have my photos printed that size and scrapbook around them, rather than plan a page and then decide what picture size will work for it. Since I already have the pictures *ready* to go, I'm more likely to get to work!"

—LISA TRUESDELL

Soupe Aux Monstres | sophie trahan

Supplies *Cardstock:* Bazzill Basics Paper, Prism Papers and Canson; *Patterned paper, brads and felt flowers:* American Crafts; *Epoxy sticker:* Bobarbo; *Ink:* Tim Holtz Distress Ink, Ranger Industries; *Pen:* Uni-ball Signo, Sanford; *Paint:* FolkArt, Plaid Enterprises; *Fonts:* Rage Italic, Microsoft; Freestyle Script, downloaded from the Internet.

"I find that *lining* up my pictures in a very organized way is usually quite eye-pleasing and effective design-wise. And allowing some pictures to span both pages of my layout opened up a whole new *array* of possibilities!"

—SOPHIE TRAHAN

All My Children | beth opel

Supplies *Cardstock:* Prism Papers; *Patterned paper:* Bo-Bunny Press and Cross-My-Heart; *Rub-ons:* Die Cuts With a View (stitches), KI Memories (numbers) and Making Memories (letters); *Acrylic flowers:* KI Memories; *Chipboard letters:* Heidi Swapp for Advantus; *Button:* Doodlebug Design; *Liquid appliqué:* Making Memories; *Font:* Arial Narrow, Microsoft.

When *focusing* on people and not an event, use close-up shots to let their personalities show on your layout.

Miami Beach | erin lincoln

Supplies *Patterned paper:* KI Memories; *Circle die cut:* QuicKutz; *Paint:* Making Memories; *Punch:* EK Success; *Fonts:* Uptown Neon, downloaded from the Internet; Times New Roman, Microsoft.

Cousins | stephanie vetne

Supplies *Digital patterned paper:* Stephanie's own designs; *Digital grunge overlay and clock:* Katie Pertiet, www.designerdigitals.com; *Digital ribbon:* Echoes of Asia Kit by Jessica Sprague, www.creatingkeepsakes.com; *Digital epoxy embellishments:* Pattie Knox, www.designerdigitals.com; *Font:* Arial, Microsoft.

photo

catalog

I love displaying photos on my desk, and a handy photo file, like a Rolodex or similar revolving file system, makes it fun and creative! I altered a file system to create a quick catalog of my favorite photos. The chipboard index cards are 4″ x 6″, which makes them ideal for displaying horizontal photos.

Here's how:

1. Embellish the tabs with patterned papers, category names and small decorative accents.

2. Using the blank file cards as a template, crop your photos to fit and adhere them to the file cards.

3. Add the cards to the file system.

4. If desired, use label stickers to add captions or notes to your photos.

Variation: This is a great gift for parents and grandparents. Consider making a personalized photo file of your favorite photos of your children. Or, catalog your favorite photos of the people, places and things that make you happy and keep it on your desk for when you need a little pick-me-up.

—by vanessa hoy

Love File | vanessa hoy

Supplies *File system:* Scrap-O-Dex, Zsiage; *Patterned paper and chipboard cover:* Die Cuts With a View; *Word stickers:* Heidi Grace Designs; *Paint:* Making Memories and Delta Creative; *Chipboard phrase, hearts and flower accents:* Fancy Pants Designs; *Ribbon:* Lasting Impressions for Paper.

accordion photo card

Photo mailers are great timesavers. They allow me to personalize cards with 4" x 6" prints when I don't have the time (or energy!) to design cards from scratch. But what if I want to share a bunch of photos? An accordion-style photo card is a great solution. I used the Overton House Designs photo mailer by EK Success along with 4" x 6" premade overlays by Making Memories to quickly create this photo card to share the news and photos of our newest family member, Jack. Here's how:

① Insert photos into the card mailer (it works best to use vertical prints).

② To add color and visual interest without adding a lot of extra weight or bulk to the card, use rub-ons and transparencies to embellish.

Variation: An accordion-style photo mailer is a great way to tell a quick story. Plus, it's great for sending vacation photos. Just add blank label stickers to fill in with captions or notes from your trip.

—by vanessa hoy

Thinking of You Card | vanessa hoy
photos by chris hoy

Supplies *Photo mailer and envelope:* Overton House
Designs, EK Success; *Transparent overlays:* Making
Memories; *Rub-on doodles and phrases:* Déjà Views,
The C-Thru Ruler Co.; *Pen:* Close To My Heart.

Teenagers love to display photos of their friends. Here's a stylish way for them to show them off and change them as often as they'd like. The best part is you can customize this piece of decor to match your teenager's room.

how to make this:

> Spray paint a baker's rack and set it aside to dry.

> Adhere felt, flowers and ribbon to binder clips and attach them to the baker's rack.

try this too:

Try embellishing clothespins as clips or using a different-shaped baker's rack to hang the photos on.

—by britney mellen

photo display

rack

Memories in Bloom | britney mellen

Supplies *Felt, buttons, spray paint and rickrack:* Jo-Ann Scrap Essentials; *Flowers and brads:* Making Memories; *Other:* Baker's rack.

lisa bearnson

from camera to composition

Here's a little expert advice from Lisa on creating layouts with 4" x 6" photos. Follow her creative process in this Q & A to see how she puts a layout together.

Q **What is the story behind these pictures?**

A Becky Higgins and I were in Philadelphia, so her husband, David; my husband, Steve and son, Kade, decided to go to New York City for the day. It turned out to be a nightmare of a day! It was very cold, very crowded and they got lost several times!

Kade and Steve

Way too cold!

Q **How did you choose the photos you used on this layout?**

A I used all of the photos that were taken that day. I couldn't leave any out because together they told the complete story.

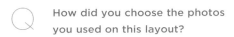

Toy shopping . . . at last!

Q **How did you choose the colors and embellishments for your layout?**

A I always start with the photos and then choose papers that match them. I kept my embellishments to a minimum—I really wanted the photos and journaling to be the stars of the layout.

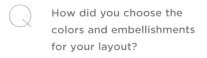

Touring the city

According to David Higgins:

(Kade's 10th Birthday—
December 28, 2000)

Lisa and Becky had a QVC show in Philly, so Steve, Kade and I decided to go to NYC for the day.

We decided the best way to get to NYC was to drive to Newark, then take the train to the city. After an hour of driving, we discovered we were going the wrong way. So, we turned around and drove another hour to get back to where we started, then another hour and a half to get to the train station. We finally got to NYC at 12:30 p.m. and discovered it was the coldest day ever—way below zero with a high wind chill factor. We had to accomplish two things in New York (Kade's request for his birthday): Lunch at Jeckyl & Hyde's and a visit to FAO Schwartz.

By this time it was lunchtime, so we decided to go to Jeckyl & Hyde right away. Steve called information to get the address. We walked 15 blocks and changed trains four times only to find out we were at the wrong Jeckyl & Hyde!

By this time we were starving, but Kade was determined to go to the real Jeckyl & Hyde. So we walked and rode back to Point A (in the 20-below-zero weather) and found Jeckyl & Hyde a few blocks away. It conveniently had an hour and a half wait. We ended up eating in a deli across the street while watching everyone else wait in line. Steve and I went very happy Kade made that compromise.

Our next adventure was to FAO Schwartz. We approached the store to discover the hour-long wait just to get inside the store! Out of frustration, Kade and I darted in the exit door. After discovering Steve wasn't with us, we waited a few minutes and went to the front door and said, "This boy has lost his father." (We could see Steve at this point, not wanting to butt in line.) We all got in and spent many hours in a very crowded FAO Schwartz.

At the end of the day, we agreed this was the worst day ever. But, it also was the best day ever. We hysterically laugh everytime we see these photos and recall this miserable time.

NYC Fiasco | lisa bearnson

Supplies *Letter die cuts:* Cricut, Provo Craft; *Snowflake accents:* Heidi Swapp for Advantus; *Font:* Tahoma, Microsoft.

Ask your photo *subjects* to strike the same pose and snap a group photo. Then take individual shots of each person—it will give you many fun options to scrapbook!

layouts
with

8 OR MORE

photos

Brodey you had a blast on your first trip to the zoo! You loved seeing all the animals & Mumu even got to go! The zoo was our favorite hangout for the

The Zoo | April Massad

Supplies *Cardstock:* Bo-Bunny Press; *Patterned paper and chipboard letters:* BasicGrey; *Word stamps:* KI Memories; *Pen:* Zig Writer, EK Success; *Ink:* Bazzill Basics Paper (blue) and StazOn, Tsukineko (black); *Adhesive:* EZ Runner, Scrapbook Adhesives by 3L; Glue Stick and Foam Adhesive Squares, The Paper Studio. **Bright idea:** Punch three circles from patterned paper. Cut the largest in half and tuck it under the journaling strip at left. Stamp words on the other two circles and elevate them with adhesive dots.

FINISH IT FASTER!
Create your own "fur" designs with ink and paper.

Get **"ZOO-RIFIC"** results with four photos on the top and six below. Add a journaling strip between rows and a patterned-paper strip above and below. Go a little **"WILD"** and ink and outline your title letters.

Winter Fun | Kim Blackinton

Supplies *Cardstock:* Crate Paper (green) and Die Cuts With a View (blue); *Patterned paper and arrow tag:* Scenic Route; *Wood tag:* Chatterbox; *Letter stickers:* American Crafts; *Flowers:* Prima; *Brads:* Making Memories; *Adhesive:* Glue Dots International and Scrapbook Adhesives by 3L. **Bright idea:** Switch up the photos, journaling block and title block to create a fresh, new look.

FINISH IT FASTER!
Help draw the eye with a no-fuss arrow tag.

Grand Staircase, Escalante
Dry Fork of Coyote Gulch &
Peek-a-Boo Gulch

This was one of the best hikes I have been on. We drove down to Torrey and spent the night at a relative's house. Got up early the next morning and hiked all day in Escalante and drove home. It was beautiful driving over the Boulder Mountains and stopping to look at the view. Spectacular! While we hike down in Coyote Gulch we didn't see much wildlife but a jackrabbit and the nest of an eagle. No rushing water since it was February and it was still really cold. No snow was going to melt at the time. We explored and took lots of pictures. I really want to go back and explore some different places around there. One day was not enough.

good times

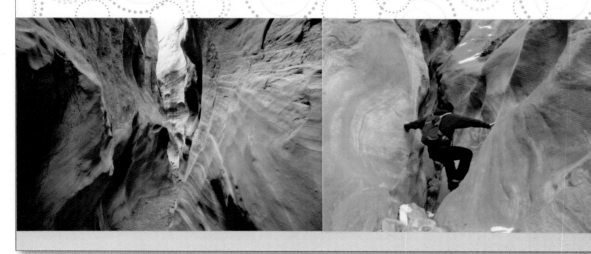

Choose a subtle contrasting cardstock to keep the **FOCUS** on the photos. Create a 4" x 6" journaling block and adorn it with brads. Line up five 4" x 6" photos and the journaling block across the top of the layout (slightly overlapping the edges). Add three 6" wide horizontal photos at bottom right. To visually separate the rows of photos, adhere a strip of patterned paper between them. Cut cardstock for a title block at bottom left. **FINISH** up with a tag, ribbon, flowers, letter stickers and a brad.

Ballgame | Lori Anderson

Supplies *Cardstock:* Wausau Paper; *Ribbon:* American Crafts; *Brads:* Making Memories; *Fonts:* Cambria, CK Soccer Mom, Constantia and Marcelle Script; *Adhesives:* Therm O Web and Tombow; *Other:* Staple and tickets. **Bright idea:** To keep blocked photos from "meshing" in a tight space, request that they be printed with white borders.

FINISH IT FASTER!
Replace the ribbon and brads with a strip of patterned paper.

For it's one, two, three strikes you're out

at the old
Ballgame

We were lucky that Dad was able to get some Salt Lake Bees tickets from someone at his work. It's not often that we can all go downtown and catch a game. It was a gorgeous summer night, and we decided to ride the Frontrunner train for the first time as a family (although, we missed Zack. He was in St. George with Grandma and Grandpa). In the Frontrunner parking lot, Josh was trying to hurry out of the car and took a nosedive into the pavement. He was a trooper and was still able to make the trip. After we made it downtown, we boarded Trax and made our way to Franklin Covey Field. The kids loved every minute of the trip. The highlight was seeing the Bees' mascot and the fireworks after the game. It was a long game to sit through, but the treats kept all of us busy. Baseball is one sport that the whole family loves. We need to be sure to try to do this every year!

Don't feel like you have to dress up your pages with "stuff." Often, your **BEAUTIFUL** photos already dress up the space on their own. Adhere photos, then add ribbon and brads to a decorative block of cardstock at bottom right. Type and format journaling on your computer, then adhere the resulting journaling block over the ribbon and between the brads. Staple and adhere baseball tickets together, then attach them to the layout with **DIMENSIONAL** adhesive.

Soccer | summer fullerton

Supplies *Cardstock:* Bazzill Basics Paper; *Patterned paper, stickers and rub-ons:* Reminisce; *Chipboard letters:* BasicGrey; *Paint:* Plaid Enterprises; *Pen:* American Crafts; *Font:* Century Gothic, Microsoft.

Creating a *sports* layout? Mix action shots with posed photographs for visual interest.

"Whenever I'm out taking *pictures* of my family during a trip, I always remind myself to take a variety of shots—ones where the subjects aren't always in the center of the frame! It's an easy way to get interesting shots, and it's great way to *create* journaling space directly on your photographs."

—VANESSA HOY

My Everything Girl | stephanie vetne

Supplies *Digital patterned paper:* Flutter Butter Kit by Mindy Terasawa and Vintage Garden Paper Pack by Dana Zarling, *www.designerdigitals.com*; *Digital embellishments:* Postage Strips, Scribbled-n-Scripted Shapes and Metal-Rimmed Epoxies Sweet Thoughts by Katie Pertiet, *www.designerdigitals.com*; *Digital quote:* Butterfly Kisses by Rhonna Farrer, *www.twopeasinabucket.com*; *Fonts:* Chocolate Box Decorative, downloaded from the Internet; Arial, Microsoft.

Fickle | amanda probst

Supplies *Cardstock:* Bazzill Basics Paper; *Fonts:* Arial and Impact, Microsoft.

Answers: 1. 2004 2. 2006 3. 2005 4. 2005 5. 2003 6. 2004 7. 2003 8. 2005 9. 2006

What Year Was It? | denine zielinski

Supplies *Cardstock:* Bazzill Basics Paper (brown) and Die Cuts With a View (blue); *Patterned paper:* KI Memories; *Letter stickers:* BasicGrey; *Metal-rimmed tags:* EK Success; *Number stickers:* Die Cuts With a View; *Ink:* ColorBox, Clearsnap; *Square punch:* Marvy Uchida; *Fonts:* Modern No. 20, downloaded from the Internet; Century Gothic, Microsoft.

Use a *square* punch to isolate photographs of your subject.

Fountain Techniques | beth opel

Supplies *Cardstock:* Prism Papers (aqua), Die Cuts With a View (periwinkle) and Bazzill Basics Paper (blue); *Patterned paper:* Flair Designs; *Epoxy letters:* KI Memories; *Brads:* Making Memories; *Circle punches:* EK Success; *Embossing marker and heat tool:* Marvy Uchida; *Embossing powder:* Top Boss, Clearsnap; *Font:* AL Uncle Charles, downloaded from *www.twopeasinabucket.com*.

"I've *found* that when I scrapbook with 4" x 6" photos, I'm more productive. I have a lot of fun challenging myself to find new ways to *arrange* my layouts."

—MICHELLE TORNAY

On the Boat | erin lincoln

Supplies *Patterned paper:* BasicGrey and Scenic Route; *Stickers and chipboard backets:* BasicGrey; *Stamp:* FontWerks; *Brads:* American Crafts and Making Memories; *Photo corners:* QuicKutz; *Font:* AL Uncle Charles, downloaded from *www.twopeasina-bucket.com; Other:* Ink.

No time in recent memory have I enjoyed a moment in time so much. Two days up at the lake this summer spent on a 20 foot Ebbtide with my family, turning perfectly good diesel fuel into noise. I'll spend the next 12 months dreaming of jumping off the back of the boat, into the water...laughing at our crazy attempts at water sports...cruising along, bumping along the wakes...taking pride in my captain of a husband. Seriously. It was perfect. I want to go back. NOW.

"I used to spend too much *time* setting up the perfect still-life shots to support my lay-outs. Then one day I realized I should spend less time on the perfect shot and more time just *enjoying* life. So, I take a couple of shots and—even if they're not perfect—I move on. Even the non-perfect photos will help me tell my story on a layout."

—BRITTANY BEATTIE

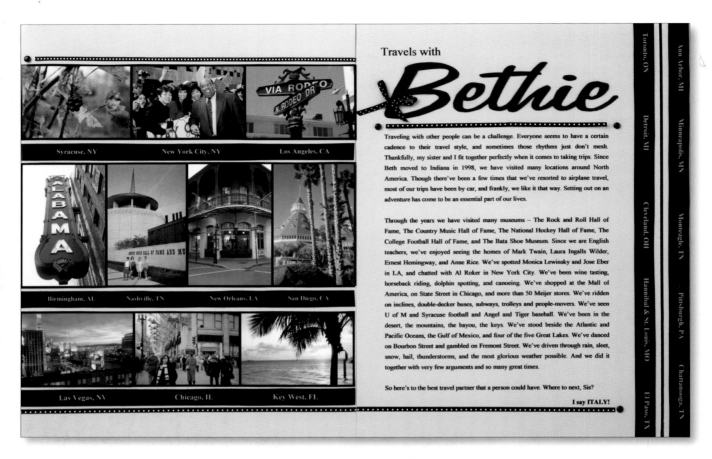

Travels with Bethie | susan opel

Supplies *Cardstock:* Bazzill Basics Paper; *Ribbon:* Mrs. Grossman's; *Adhesive strip:* KI Memories; *Brads:* Heidi Swapp for Advantus; *Fonts:* Jott45 ("Bethie"), downloaded from the Internet; Times New Roman (journaling), Microsoft.

"When I take a short weekend *trip* with my daughter, I'll sometimes just stop at the store and buy each of us a disposable camera. At the end of our trip, it's fun to drop the cameras off at a local photo lab and request double prints. When the prints come back, we've got a great assortment of prints from both of our perspectives and we can both pick and choose which *stories* we most want to scrapbook."

—RACHEL THOMAE

At the Zoo | april peterson

Supplies *Cardstock:* Bazzill Basics Paper; *Patterned paper:* My Mind's Eye and Chatterbox; *Chipboard letters:* American Crafts; *Chipboard tags and epoxy stickers:* Making Memories; *Brads:* Queen & Co.; *Stamp:* CherryArte; *Ink:* ColorBox, Clearsnap; *Letter die cuts:* QuickKutz.

ORGANIZED

I'm aware that I'm a pretty darn organized gal. I love stacks, lineups, compartments, and systems. I devour home-improvement programs like *Clean Sweep*, *neat*, and *Mission: Organization*. My spices and CDs are in alphabetical order. My scrapbook storage is a paradise of baskets, boxes, and bins. Collections from cosmetics to clothes are sorted by color. I adore products from The Container Store and Hold Everything.

People who hear of my penchant for order often tell me that I have too much time on my hands. Actually, that's not at all true. The time I expend creating my methods and structures is gained back a hundredfold by being able to know exactly where everything belongs!

However, I'm working on letting go just a little now and then. Occasionally I don't make my bed all day. I've actually left clothes out overnight. And guess what? The world didn't come to an end! Life doesn't always come in neatly organized compartments, and I want to be a little more flexible. But you gotta admit that it's awfully pretty my way!

get it together

Organized | beth opel

Supplies *Cardstock:* Bazzill Basics Paper; *Paper flowers:* Prima; *Epoxy sticker and ribbon:* KI Memories; *Brads:* Creative Impressions; *Fonts:* Beau (journaling), downloaded from *www.dafont.com*; Twentieth Century Condensed (title), Microsoft.

"Because I *print* all my photos on the computer, I can crop or resize them. Still, I choose 4" x 6" or smaller because I like to use a lot of photos on one page to really give a wide overview of my *topic* or event."

—BETH OPEL

Joy | susan opel

Supplies *Cardstock:* KI Memories and Bazzill Basics Paper; *Patterned paper, ribbon, chipboard accents and brads:* KI Memories; *Rub-ons:* American Crafts.

"While on vacation, I look for *unique* albums for scrapbooking my travel photographs. Last year, I picked up a handcrafted 5" x 7" album created by a local artist. When I got home, I was *excited* to upload my photographs, print them and place them in the album. My 4" x 6" prints required no cropping and allowed just enough room for a sentence or two of handwritten journaling."

—RACHEL THOMAE

New Friends | stephanie vetne

Supplies *Digital ribbon, stickers and tags:* Desert Blooms Kit by Mindy Terasawa, *www.designerdigitals.com; Fonts:* Chocolate Box and Edwardian Script, downloaded from the Internet.

& OLD TRAINS

ALMOST 4

A *quick* way to create a 10-photo layout? Arrange four horizontal 4" x 6" photos along the top of your layout and six vertical 4" x 6" photos along the bottom!

Seeing El Salvador | leah la montagne
Supplies *Rub-ons:* Chartpak; *Brads:* Queen & Co.; *Pen:* Pigma Micron, Sakura; *Other:* Cardstock.

Place your focal-point *photo* in the center of your layout on a colorful background (here, a color wheel), then use brads to lead the eye to it.

"Whether I'm on *vacation* with my family or just on a day trip with my husband and dogs, I always make sure I take my turn in front of the camera. That way, my scrapbook albums can *capture* the fact that I was there too!"

—VANESSA HOY

The Rocky Mountain National Park had a Junior Park Ranger program. Got the boys the little booklets with assigned activities (scavenger hunts, recycling questions, homework of picking up litter, etc.). Hiked around Bear Lake looking for plants and animals. Went to Sprague Lake for a Ranger led program. The boys followed the Ranger (Keri) and the other kids as they talked about habitats, pointed out trees, learned to recognize trees by feel, and pretended to horde food for the winter. They had such a good time and got their booklets signed. We took them to the Alpine Visitor Center so the boys could receive their official Junior Park Ranger badge for completing the booklet and program. So proud.
- mid-August 2006

Junior Park Rangers | amanda probst
Supplies *Cardstock:* Bazzill Basics Paper; *Patterned paper and brads:* American Crafts; *Ribbon:* Li'l Davis Designs; *Font:* Eurostile, downloaded from the Internet.

Field Trip | sara wise

Supplies *Cardstock:* Bazzill Basics Paper; *Patterned paper:* Scenic Route; *Star brads:* Making Memories; *Stamps:* Chronicle Books, Junkitz, Hero Arts (quote) and Sassafras Lass (stitching); *Ink:* Tim Holtz Distress Ink, Ranger Industries; *Label tape:* Dymo; *Chipboard letters:* Pressed Petals; *White painter's pen:* Elmer's; *Ledger tab stamps:* Autumn Leaves; *Paint:* Apple Barrel, Plaid Enterprises; *Font:* SP Coffee Break, downloaded from *www.scrapsupply.com*.

Images of Italy | tracy odachowski

Supplies *Cardstock:* Bazzill Basics Paper; *Patterned paper:* BasicGrey; *Patterned-paper overlay:* Hambly Studios; *Fonts:* Antigoni ("Images of") and Carpenter ICG ("Italy"), Microsoft.

The Hunt | wendy anderson

Supplies *Patterned paper:* Making Memories; *Letter stickers:* Three Bugs in a Rug; *Ribbon:* Making Memories; *Rubber "Easter" accent:* Doodlebug Design; *Metal photo corner and pen:* American Crafts; *Square punch:* Marvy Uchida.

Looking for a photo display that Dad will love? Adhere your 4" x 6" photos to book-ends for a masculine yet personal display he's sure to enjoy.

how to make this:

> Trim your photos to fit your chosen bookends.

> Adhere your photos using a decoupage medium.

> Embellish the photos to match your decor.

try this too:

Look around the house for other items you can personalize with photos. You can attach photos to a wooden cigar box the same way you attach photos to bookends.

—britney mellen

book-ends

Bookends for Dad | britney mellen
Supplies *Decoupage medium:* Mod Podge, Plaid Enterprises;
Other: Bookends.

SKETCHES FOR 4" X 6" PHOTOS

Start your layouts with a plan

Sketches can be an important part of the scrapbooking process. They serve as a visual "map," showing the placement of photos and elements, therefore eliminating the guesswork and saving precious minutes while you scrapbook. Sketches are great for the organized scrapbooker who likes to begin with the end in mind. They are also perfect for those of us who have found ourselves "stuck in a rut" and need to jump start our creativity again.

We've created 27 sketches that were inspired by layouts found in this book and compiled them here, so you'll have lots of ideas at your fingertips.

Don't forget to try rotating a sketch to mix it up a bit. Or, add or subtract additional elements from the design for a different look. That's part of the fun!

1 TO 2 PHOTOS

Share | Laina Lamb
Page 17

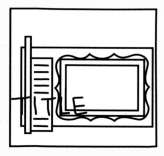

Couch | Lisa Kisch
Page 19

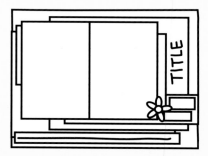

Happy Together | Emily Spahn
Page 23

Sleepy Head | Lisa Truesdell
Page 24

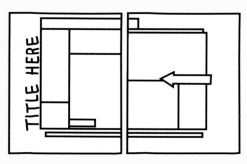

Are We There Yet | Mou Saha
Page 26

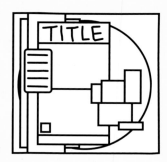

Garden Fresh | Lisa Swift
Page 30

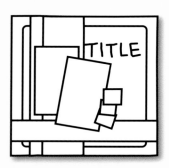

Bathing Beauty | Kathi Kirkland
Page 40

Yeehah | Heidi Sonboul
Page 35

Follow Your Dreams | Laina Lamb
Page 45

3 TO 4 PHOTOS

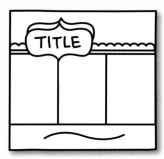

Butterfly Kisses | Suzy Plantamura
Page 86

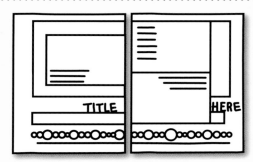

Apple of Our Eyes | Mou Saha
Page 87

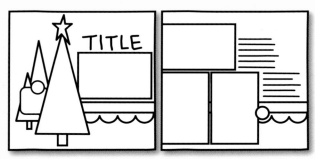

Our Santa Visit Gone Bad | Allison Davis
Page 112

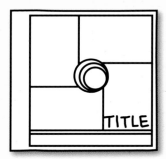

Johnny Rockets | Kelly Purkey
Page 115

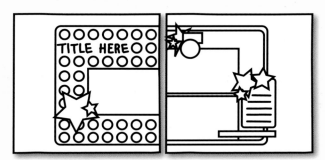

My Adorable Boys | Allison Davis
Page 92

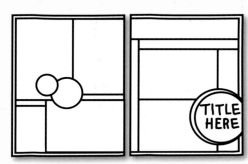

Clam Chowder for Lunch | Kelly Purkey
Page 118

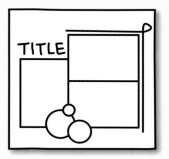

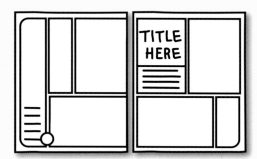

Sandy | Katie Anaya
Page 97

Horse Back Ride | Ria Mojica
Page 96

Blue Ice Cream | Beth Opel
Page 124

5 OR MORE PHOTOS

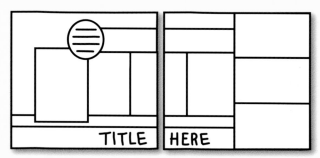

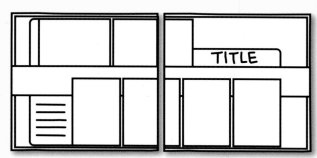

Halloween 2007 | Katie Anaya
Page 182

Bronze | Jill Paulson
Page 184

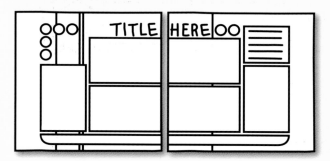

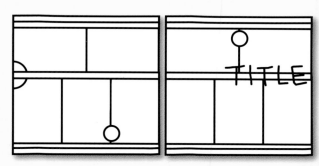

First and Last | Allison Davis
Page 186

The Zoo | April Massad
Page 218

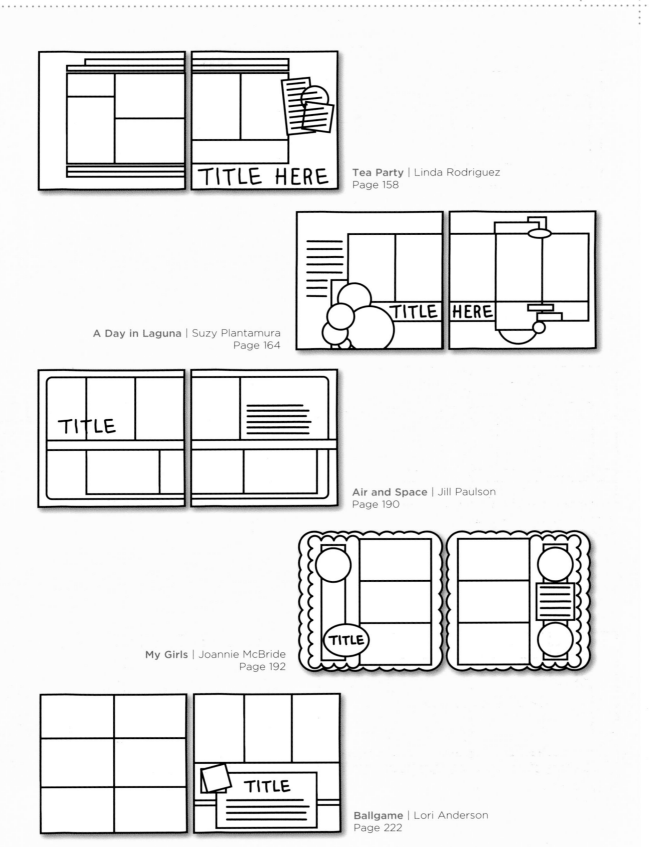

Tea Party | Linda Rodriguez
Page 158

A Day in Laguna | Suzy Plantamura
Page 164

Air and Space | Jill Paulson
Page 190

My Girls | Joannie McBride
Page 192

Ballgame | Lori Anderson
Page 222

mini
albums
with

4x6

photos

envelope mini book

Create a clever album using envelopes as the base, then store tags or hidden journaling in the pockets!

April **says:** "Remember those paper-bag mini albums that were so popular a year or two ago? I've created an alternative that's quick, easy and inexpensive. To create this project, I sealed two 4" x 9½" envelopes closed and cut them in half to create four 4" x 4¾" pieces. Then, I trimmed my photos and adhered them to the envelopes (open side on top). After creating a front and back cover with two pieces, I punched two sets of holes in each decorated envelope and threaded them together with ribbon for the binding."

Variation: Mini books created from tags or envelopes are great as interactive gifts. Give one as a birthday present and slip sweet notes and gift cards in the pockets!

Birthday Party Album | april peterson

Supplies *Cardstock:* Bazzill Basics Paper; *Patterned paper and stickers:* My Mind's Eye; *Circular stickers and tabs:* 7gypsies; *Ribbon:* Making Memories (blue), KI Memories (green) and May Arts (orange); *Metal letters:* KI Memories; *Chipboard number:* BasicGrey; *Envelopes:* Waste Not Paper.

fill-in baby album

Working with one line of patterned paper and coordinating cardstock will help save time when creating a gift fill-in album. Another great timesaver? Repeat the same elements—accents, stitching, etc.—on each page.

Mary **says:** "With our baby due in a few short weeks, I planned this album for the photos I would take of family and friends with our new son or daughter. I know I'll have a lot of cherished photos, but I don't want to spend a lot of time writing journaling, so I left space so that each person can write his or her own thoughts or a simple welcome to the baby."

Variation: Create a fill-in album before a big event, such as a bridal shower, wedding anniversary or graduation party.

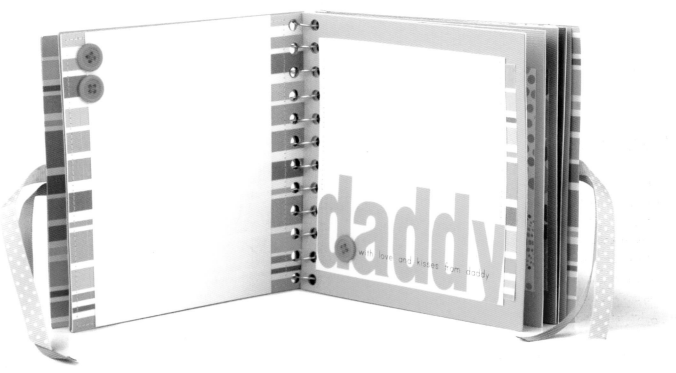

Love Baby Album | mary macaskill

Supplies *Cardstock:* Bazzill Basics Paper; *Patterned paper, coasters and cotton art tape:* Gin-X, Imagination Project; *Ribbon:* C.M. Offray & Son and American Crafts; *Buttons:* JHB Buttons; *Rub-ons:* American Crafts; *Fonts:* Haettenschweiler, downloaded from the Internet; Print Clearly, downloaded from *www.dafont.com*.

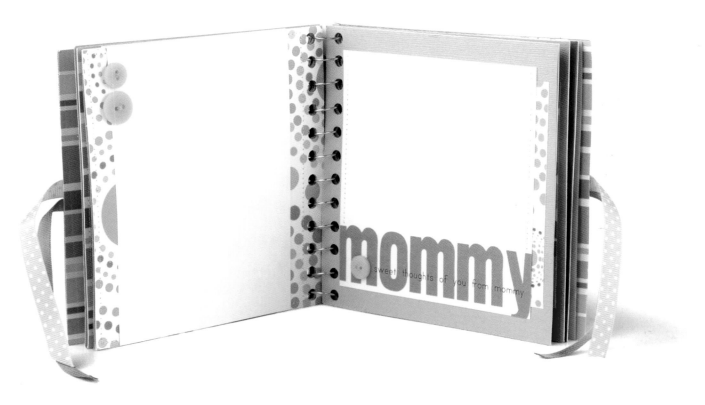

photo journal

Slip photos into a mini album or photo album and use label stickers to highlight or add captions to your photos.

Ali **says:** "Last year I took a trip to Tokyo and managed to take a lot of photos. (Can you believe that?) One of the cool things I noticed right away was that I was attracted to a wide variety of textures in the environment. In addition to a larger travel album, I wanted to create a special home just for these texture photos. I love how they tell their own story about my adventures!"

Variation: When you go on a trip, share the experience from a different perspective. Have your child take photos with a disposable camera and create a quick mini book from his point of view. Or, take close-ups shots of all the places you visit, from sand on the beach to the texture on an old historic building.

Tokyo Textures Album | ali edwards
Supplies *Album:* Kokuyo; *Rub-ons:* American Crafts; *Transparency:* Hambly Studios; *Blank label stickers:* 7gypsies.

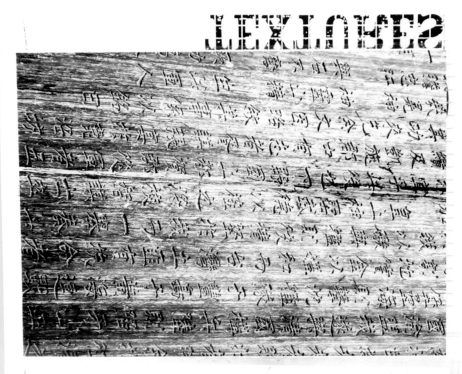

TOKYO 2008 One of the first things that was totally cool about tokyo were all the textures — both "real people" and objects. My camera was busy capturing so many different patterns and textures that kept appearing all over the place. Anything with characters was very textural (especially since I can't read). Such a cool experience to capture.

artistic mini album

Want your 4" x 6" photos to really stand out in your mini album? Opt for a smaller page size. Allison loved the illusion of enlargements on her 6" x 6" pages without having to use as many supplies to complete artistic and unique designs.

Allison **says:** "I wanted to create something just for fun—with no purpose to the album other than just to create. A 6" x 6" album allowed me to finish each page quickly and create something frivolous. I figured it was so small that I could make pages on just about anything."

Variation: Before enlarging your favorite photo for a layout, try Allison's idea using the original 4" x 6" print. It's a perfect solution for a gift album—and can also spark your creativity when creating a layout on a larger scale!

Daily Dose | allison kimball

Supplies *Album:* American Crafts; *Chipboard letters:* Heidi Swapp for Advantus ("A") and Scenic Route (all others); *Rub-on letters:* BasicGrey; *Ribbon:* Strano Designs; *Ink:* Clearsnap; *Other:* Red stars.

Album Introduction | allison kimball

Supplies *Patterned paper:* KI Memories and Scenic Route; *Striped tag and reinforcements:* KI Memories; *Square tab and rub-on quote:* 7gypsies; *Ink:* ColorBox Fluid Chalk, Clearsnap; *Chipboard "K":* Scenic Route; *Other:* Flower, ribbon and square tag.

Today I Leaned | allison kimball

Supplies *Cardstock with die-cut window:* Making Memories; *Tag:* My Mind's Eye; *Ink:* ColorBox Fluid Chalk, Clearsnap; *Rub-ons:* KI Memories; *Date stamp:* OfficeMax; *Other:* Ribbon.

Love at Home | allison kimball

Supplies *Tree design (with circles and heart):* Allison's own design; *Patterned paper:* BasicGrey; *Printed tag:* Making Memories; *Striped tab:* EK Success; *Rub-ons:* 7gypsies; *Date stamp:* OfficeMax; *Ink:* ColorBox Fluid Chalk, Clearsnap; *Other:* Ribbon.

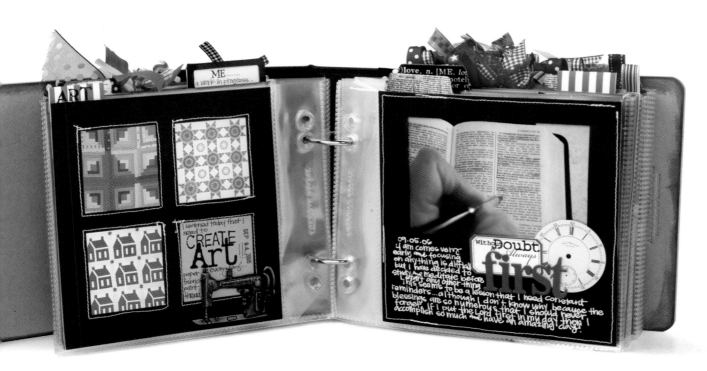

Create Art | allison kimball

Supplies *Cardstock with die-cut windows:* Making Memories; *Rub-ons:* Autumn Leaves; *Sewing-machine charm:* K&Company; *Quilt designs:* From a quilting book (title unknown); *Date stamp:* OfficeMax; *Other:* Thread.

First | allison kimball

Supplies *Cardstock with die-cut window:* Making Memories; *Tab:* Daisy D's Paper Co.; *Label and clock:* Li'l Davis Designs; *Chipboard letters:* Heidi Swapp for Advantus; *White pen:* Uni-ball Signo, Sanford; *Rub-ons:* 7gypsies; *Other:* Thread.

7 Days | allison kimball

Supplies *Patterned paper:* K&Company; *Chipboard number:* Junkitz; *Chipboard letters:* Heidi Swapp for Advantus; *Date stamp:* OfficeMax; *Border sticker:* KI Memories; *Other:* Ribbon.

Chocolate | allison kimball

Supplies *Tab:* EK Success; *Border sticker:* KI Memories; *Decorative tape:* Heidi Swapp for Advantus; *Ink:* ColorBox Fluid Chalk, Clearsnap; *Rub-ons:* Autumn Leaves.

Get It Together | allison kimball

Supplies *Die-cut patterned paper:* Making Memories; *"A" die cut:* BasicGrey; *Ink:* ColorBox Fluid Chalk, Clearsnap; *Chipboard checkmarks:* Corners cut from chipboard packaging; *Printed quote and gel sticker:* KI Memories; *Tab:* Daisy D's Paper Co.; *Rub-ons:* Autumn Leaves; *Other:* Thread.

Strengths | allison kimball

Supplies *Patterned paper:* American Crafts; *Reinforcements:* KI Memories; *Lined stamp:* FontWerks; *Ink:* ColorBox Fluid Chalk, Clearsnap; *Letter stickers:* Doodlebug Design; *Other:* Tag and ribbon.

I Love You Even Though . . . | allison kimball

Supplies *Tab and "I Love You" sticker:* Heidi Grace Designs; *Letter stickers:* American Crafts; *"Devoted" tab and rub-ons:* 7gypsies; *Ink:* ColorBox Fluid Chalk, Clearsnap; *Newspaper flower:* Junkitz; *Other:* Thread.

"Scrapbooking with 4" x 6" photos is *great!* They are the staple of my layouts and mini albums. You can line them up, crop them into a collage or just use one for visual *impact*."

—ALLISON KIMBALL

keepsake gift album

Make memorable keepsake albums with creative packaging! Creasa created this beautiful album of her favorite photos and stored it in a wooden box she decorated to match.

Creasa **says:** "When I have a lot of similar pictures I just love, I print them out as 4" x 6" prints, scrap them in a mini album and store the album in a decorative box. These are also fun to create for holidays when I have too many pictures to fit on a 12" x 12" layout!"

Variation: Cute packaging comes in all shapes and sizes. The next time you find a mint or candy tin you love, consider the tiny albums or accordion-style mini books you can make to tuck inside.

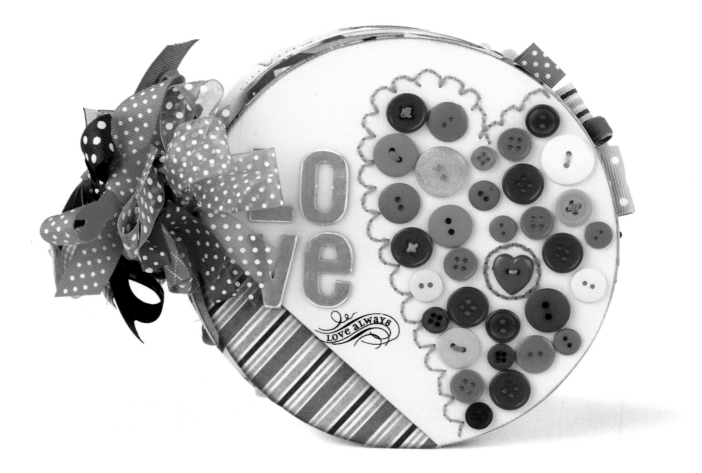

Love Always | creasa brown

Supplies *Box:* Lu-Yi Wood; *Cardstock:* Bazzill Basics Paper; *Patterned paper, letter stickers and chipboard:* BasicGrey; *Buttons:* Making Memories, Jesse James & Co. and Autumn Leaves; *Brads:* KI Memories and Queen & Co; *Paper flowers:* Prima; *Felt flowers:* American Crafts; *Leather flower and metal charm:* Making Memories; *Circle punch:* EK Success; *Jewels:* Making Memories, KI Memories and My Mind's Eye; *Woven label:* Karen Foster Design; *Ribbon:* Dashes, Dots & Checks; BasicGrey; KI Memories; Making Memories and C.M. Offray & Son; *Glaze:* Aleene's Instant Decoupage, Duncan Enterprises; *Ink:* VersaColor, Tsukineko; *Rub-ons:* BasicGrey, Junkitz and American Crafts; *Paper frills:* Doodlebug Design.

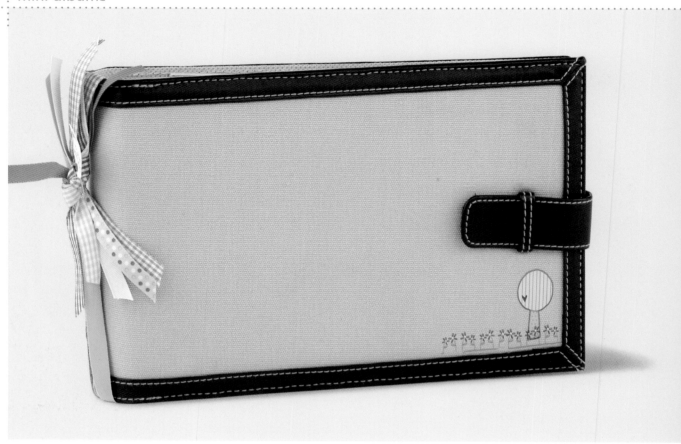

vacation mini album

If you have several photos from a vacation or special event, divide them into different categories to help you narrow down the ones that will best tell your story. Here, Wendy scrapbooked photos from a family trip to Disneyland by separating them into four categories: travel, rides, characters and other (for miscellaneous photos she wanted to include).

Wendy **says:** "When we took this vacation, I was still using a film camera, and I took about eight rolls' worth of photos! While I want to create a 12" x 12" album of all our photos and memories, I wanted to create something fun and small that the kids can look at right now."

Variation: Choosing three or four specific photo themes to include in a mini album makes creating gift albums a snap. Making an album for Mom? Choose three categories of photos you want to include, such as Mom at home, Mom with the kids and Mom having fun. It makes choosing photos simple and gives you a theme for celebrating her.

Vacation | wendy anderson

Supplies *Album:* O'Scrap!; *Cardstock:* Bazzill Basics Paper, Die Cuts With a View and Making Memories; *Patterned paper:* Heidi Grace Designs, Making Memories, Scenic Route and Sassafras Lass; *Ribbon:* O'Scrap! and American Crafts; *Rub-ons:* Heidi Grace Designs; *Safety pin:* Making Memories; *Pen:* American Crafts; *Letter die cuts:* Cricut, Provo Craft; *Other:* Tags.

Disney Princesses: Sleeping Beauty and Snow White... we waited for a long time to get these!

More Disney Girls... Alice-in Wonderland and Minnie Mouse...

all around

It was cold and rainy the entire time we were there. Luckily, we came prepared for the rain.

Even the rain couldn't douse the desire for warm churros... mmm... the best.

vacation board book

Make creating a mini album simple by choosing a basic page design for each album spread. Miriam made all her photos and journaling blocks 3″ in height. *Tip:* For a 5″ x 7″ mini book, print (or crop) vertical photos to 3″ x 2″, and horizontal photos to 3″ x 4″.

Miriam **says:** "We took over 200 photos on our family vacation to Mexico! It was such a wonderful memory for our entire family, but to scrap 12″ x 12″ pages of everything seemed like a daunting task. The beauty of a board album is that it's easy to create and is also something we can display."

Variation: Board books embellished with photos are a great way for your child to have fun and learn something, too! For example, take photos of various numbers of items to teach a child how to count.

Hola | miriam campbell

Supplies *Board book:* C&T Publishing; *Patterned paper:* BasicGrey; *Silk flower, brad (on cover) and round metal embellishments:* Imaginisce; *Metal buckle and square accents:* Nunn Design; *Chipboard letters:* Die Cuts With a View; *Lace trim and rub-ons:* Making Memories; *Ribbons:* Mrs. Grossman's; *Stitching stamp:* Rebekka Erickson for Stamp World; *Glitter:* Ice Stickles, Ranger Industries; *Ink:* Tim Holtz Distress Ink, Ranger Industries; ColorBox Fluid Chalk, Clearsnap; *Font:* American Typewriter, downloaded from the Internet. *Other:* Wooden beads.

travel-planner journal

Display 4" x 6" photos from your travels in a customizable day planner. Britney used an adaptable planner by M Book to store photos, ticket stubs and notes during a family trip to Europe.

Britney **says:** "The calendar pages and plastic sleeves were a perfect place for me to keep track of my itinerary as well as jot down notes and journal entries, and save memorabilia during our trip!"

Variation: If you don't have a premade day planner, simply add photo sleeves and calendar pages to a mini binder. This format also works well for a baby's first-year album or to track a student's school memories.

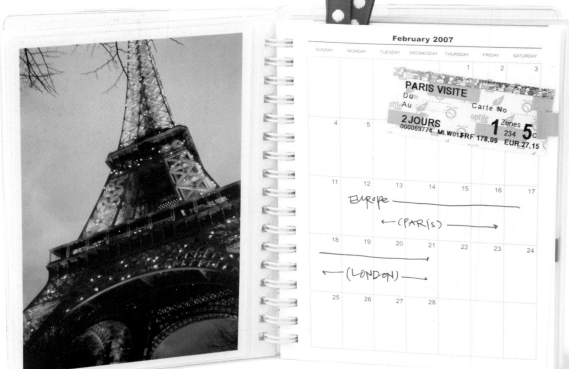

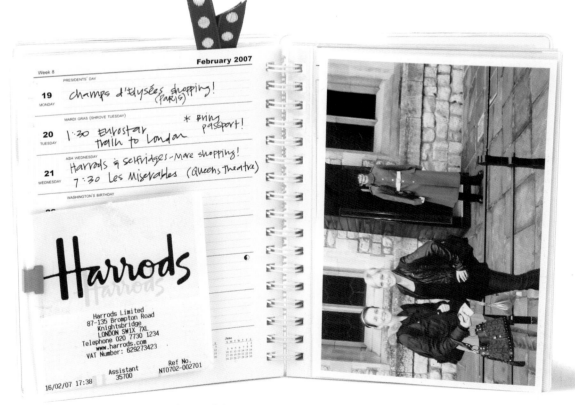

Travelogue | britney mellen

Supplies *Planner:* M Book; *Digital elements:* Love Birds Kit by Mindy Terasawa, *www.designerdigitals.com;*
Ribbon: Making Memories; *Clips:* Provo Craft; *Pen:* Pigma Micron, Sakura.

FAST ALBUMS WITH 4" X 6" PHOTOS

Scrapbook more photos in adorable—and easy!—albums.

Everyone loves looking through scrapbooks, but sometimes creating scrapbooks can seem like a daunting task. Where do you even begin? Check out the following album-making approaches to help you start (and finish) adorable albums with ease.

"People We Love" Album
Angie Lucas
Supplies: *8" x 8" album:* Pulp (custom embroidered); *Other:* Cardstock, patterned-paper scraps, brads, ribbon, ink, pen and letter stamps.

Follow a Formula

Using the same design for each page of an album is a simple way to get more photos scrapped. At first, it may feel like you're "cheating," but with the design already pre-determined, you're free to concentrate on creativity within the design. For this album, each page shows a single photo paired with patterned-paper pieces and accents, creating a pocket for the journaling card. Using different color schemes for each page and complementary patterned paper adds visual variety, so although the same design is repeated, it looks fresh on each page.

Use a Photo Album

Photo-album scrapbooking is a fun memory-keeping approach that blends the beauty of traditional scrapbooking with the speed of slipping pictures into photo sleeves. Just fill in the album's 4″ x 6″ pockets with photos, journaling blocks and pieces of patterned paper. Then add a few accents and you're done. It's a quick, creative way to get more photos off your computer or out of a box and into a book you and your family can enjoy every day.

"Smile" Album | Amy Williams

Supplies: *6″ x 8″ photo album:* MBI; *Other:* Cardstock, patterned paper, binder clips, ribbon, ink, punches, letter stickers, die-cut accents and pen.

SHOW OFF YOUR PHOTOS

Display your 4" x 6" photos for everyone to enjoy.

In addition to showcasing your favorite shots on your scrapbook pages, why not put some of them on display so they can be enjoyed on a daily basis? Check out these easy ideas for exhibiting your cherished photos. Surround yourself with the images that make you smile!

① Clip pretty images to a ribbon or wire with colorful clothespins.

② Attach frames to the front of storage boxes for a personalized look.

③

Assemble a calendar using favorite photographs from each month for the illustrations.

④

Create a stylish tote and carry your favored photos with you wherever you go!

PERFECT PRODUCTS FOR 4" X 6" PHOTOS

12 great finds for accentuating your photos

As you've seen throughout this book, super-fast doesn't mean super-plain! When you're looking for products you can use with your uncropped 4" x 6" photos, be sure to consider several different product categories: pre-cut paper, photo mats, stickers, rub-ons, stamps and more. Take a look at the following products and ideas for using them on your pages.

① Puffy Scallop Borders

American Crafts
AmericanCrafts.com
Scalloped edges give a youthful, fun look to your page—why not use them to highlight your photo? Add these puffy scallop border stickers to the 4" edges of your photo for a charming effect.

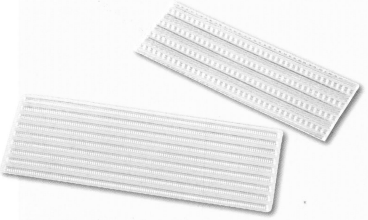

② Journaling Stamps

7gypsies
SevenGypsies.com
Add journaling lines directly below your 4" x 6" photos with the Large Clearstamp: Journal stamp set. Notice the two large, lined stamps that are sized perfectly to fit 4" x 6" photos—one vertical and one horizontal.

③ Black & White Photo Mats

Creative Memories
CreativeMemories.com
It's easy to add a little drama to your 4" x 6" photos with the Power Palette Black & White Storybox. This set includes 96 photo mats and journaling boxes. Matching patterned papers, stickers, paper frames and flowers are also available.

4

Rows of Rub-ons

Cosmo Cricket
CosmoCricket.com
You can create so many great looks with a row of these adorable rub-ons and a horizontal 4" x 6" photo. Consider applying them directly to the bottom edge of your photo, overlapping onto your background cardstock. Or, mat your photo, leaving extra room at the bottom for a row of rub-ons.

5

Title Stickers

me & my BIG ideas
MeandMyBigIdeas.com
These cute banner-style chipboard title stickers feature flocked letters and are sized just right to add above or below your horizontal 4" x 6" photo.

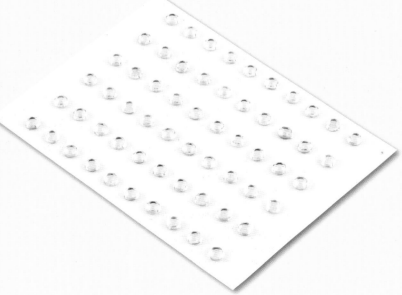

6

Gem Accents

Bazzill Basics Paper
BazzillBasics.com
Bling out your focal-point photo! Use Adhesive Jewels to add a sparkly border around your photo, or add a single jewel to each corner of your photo for delightfully dainty corner accents.

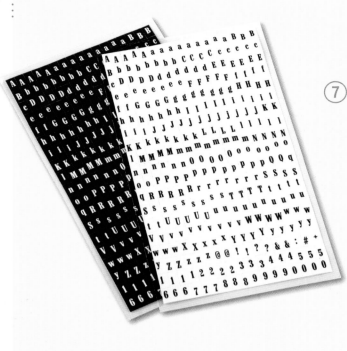

 Mini Letter Stickers

EK Success
EKSuccess.com
If you're working with a photo that has a good amount of white space, consider using Tiny Alphabet and Number Stickers to add a subtitle or caption directly to your photo. These also look great on small accent tags.

 Photo Overlays

My Mind's Eye
MyMindsEye.com
Highlight the focal-point photo on your layout with a pretty photo overlay, like these from the Penny Lane collection. Choose from full frames, bottom borders and side accents.

Flourish Stickers

Making Memories
MakingMemories.com
Give your photos a touch of elegance with these Shimmer Flourish stickers. Embellish your photo mats with several of the stickers or use just a few as graceful photo corners.

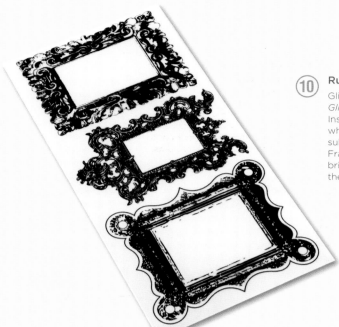

(10) **Rub-on Frames**
Glitz Design
GlitzItNow.com
Instead of cropping that photo with the extra white space around the edges, zone in on your subject with a frame accent, like these Fancy Frames rub-ons. You'll love the emphasis it brings to the subject of your photo as well as the extra stylish touch it adds to your layout.

(11)
Die-Cut Photo Mats
K&Company
KandCompany.com
Die-Cut Mat Pads make it so easy to add lovely decorative photo mats to your 4" x 6" photos. The Wild Raspberry pad features three mat shapes and 12 patterns (six double-sided designs), giving you a wonderful range of options.

(12)
Brag Book
Little Yellow Bicycle
MyLYB.com
If you have more photos than you can fit on your layout, consider adding a lightweight brag book to your page, like these from the Sharon Ann Baby Safari Collection. For a fun, interactive effect, attach them to the layout or the outside of the page protector with Velcro or thin magnets.

Take a peek back through this book as we spotlight some of our favorite ideas for 4" x 6" photos!

Crop your photos and pair them with patterned-paper strips to create page designs that flow.

page 55

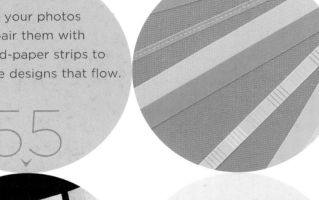

‹ Use strips of paper for a fun visual effect, leading to a special photograph.

page 52

Highlight the focus of each photo by placing a large circle on the group of photos.

page 73 ›

Put a spin on a layout by placing all of the elements at a slant. ›

page 131

Place your focal-point photo in the center of your layout on a colorful background (here, a color wheel).

page 236

‹ When creating a series of five photographs, feature one close-up of your subject for emphasis.

page 151